Progressive Atheism

RV (Pete)
- p. 22 : garbled Darwin
- how do we define all-good?
- p. 24 : folksiness
- p. 32 : thesis
- p. 41 : too small a sample
- p. 51 : what if science came first?
- p. 60 : fallacious hidden-harmony argument
- p. 83 : justified evil!

Extrapolating past a singularity (82)
The Galilean satellites (88)

Key idea: what if...
Buddha-nature
Brahman monism
Tao
... all turned out to be right (36)

- 87 what we're leaving behind

Basic Schellenberg Errors

Darwin (red in tooth and claw)

Jesus

Teresa

Evolution as progress

The False Population-Equivalence

Why privilege <u>religion</u>?

Progressive
Atheism

How Moral Evolution Changes
the God Debate

J. L. Schellenberg

BLOOMSBURY ACADEMIC
LONDON • NEW YORK • OXFORD • NEW DELHI • SYDNEY

BLOOMSBURY ACADEMIC
Bloomsbury Publishing Plc
50 Bedford Square, London, WC1B 3DP, UK
1385 Broadway, New York, NY 10018, USA

BLOOMSBURY, BLOOMSBURY ACADEMIC and the Diana logo are trademarks
of Bloomsbury Publishing Plc

First published in Great Britain 2019

Cover design by Maria Rajka
Cover image © Jose A. Bernat Bacete/Getty Images

A catalogue record for this book is available from the British Library.

A catalog record for this book is available from the Library of Congress.

ISBN: HB: 978-1-3500-9718-6
PB: 978-1-3500-9719-3
ePDF: 978-1-3500-9720-9
eBook: 978-1-3500-9721-6

Typeset by Deanta Global Publishing Services, Chennai, India
Printed and bound in Great Britain

To find out more about our authors and books visit www.bloomsbury.com
and sign up for our newsletters.

For Regina

Contents

Preface viii

1 Getting Oriented 1

2 An (A)Theological Dead End 17

3 Naturalism's Shortcut 35

4 Unexplored Territory: Moral Evolution 59

5 Updating God 77

6 A Relationally Responsive God 97

7 A Kinder God 109

8 A Nonviolent God 123

9 Challenging the New Theism 137

10 Atheism's Brave New World 155

Notes 177
Glossary 183
Acknowledgments 185
Index 186

Preface

Peeople think of me as an atheist. *I* think of me as an atheist. That's because I've defended the view that there is no personal God of the sort idealized in theistic religion. But I'm an atheist only in the relatively narrow sense just specified—the sort of atheist more commonly found in philosophy than elsewhere. In much of my work, I've been moving on from the personal God idea and exploring new religious domains, including new ways of being religious that are compatible with atheism. Indeed, this is the larger part of what I've done. Occasionally, however, I return to atheistic reasoning. I'm returning to it again in this book. I return, in part, because people won't join me in thinking about other religious topics if they're still preoccupied with theism. And in part it's because exciting new results—like the approach to atheism we'll be exploring—keep emerging in that neighborhood.

* * *

It was 2011, and a copy of Steven Pinker's book *The Better Angels of Our Nature: Why Violence Has Declined* landed with a thud at my door. Reading it, I was struck by Pinker's evidence that human empathy has grown over the years. What we see here, he suggests, is a form of moral progress opposed to violence. I remembered how I had appealed to *divine* empathy in my version of the philosophical problem of evil a few years before, and began wondering whether this sort of emphasis in the context of the God debate might get more of a grip on us today because of moral progress like that emphasized by Pinker. *Was human moral progress making us think differently about the nature of God—in particular about how a truly good God would behave—and was this opening up new possibilities of atheistic argumentation?*

It occurred to me that the hiddenness argument for atheism I had developed and defended, which was receiving a surprising amount of attention in philosophy, also fit this pattern. The hiddenness argument suggests that a common way of being undecided about the God issue itself decides the issue. Many more of us would believe in God if there were a God, since God would be supremely loving and thus open to personal relationship with beings like us. And you can't very well be open to such a relationship with someone while preventing them from believing in your existence. How inviting! The openness to relationship receiving emphasis here was something that in another time might have been shrugged off as entirely optional, especially for males and fathers. And, of course, in earlier times it would have been easier to think of God as both Male and Father. But it wasn't being shrugged off now. *Today* the hiddenness problem was a hot topic.

If there was a new pattern here, a new way of arguing atheistically, so I thought to myself, it might be a better, more powerful way of arguing than we've seen before. Perhaps it would generate new arguments, all following the same pattern. Being so different from popular atheistic approaches, which often focus on making God look bad, it might furthermore show how atheism could have a more positive and interesting role in our culture.

The seed had been planted. At various times since 2011 I've felt it there, at the back of my mind. Now, in this book, I want to see what may grow from it. What grows probably won't reach its full height here. Switching metaphors: the territory we're entering is large. The fascinating subject of human moral progress is bound up with the notion of progress in general, and that notion resides within the more general topic of cultural evolution and its mechanisms. Moreover, this general topic is only now coming into its own in science and philosophy. We're entering it at an early stage of its development. So quite a lot will be left unsaid. But I do want to open up the atheistic side of this territory for exploration. And I will do so by developing my story about God and progress as forcefully as I can in the span of these pages.

Here's a preview of the main plot line. Changes in the past few centuries, sped by developments of the past few decades, have altered our understanding of what it takes to be *a really good person*: for example, relational sensitivity and nonviolence are qualities we tend to value, in women and men alike, more deeply than humans did in the past. This is moral evolution. Moral evolution is *just* change. But if we accept the changes as right and appropriate, as clearly most of us do, we will also regard it as promoting moral progress.

Now shift over to the idea of God. The idea of God most influential in the West is the idea of an ultimate personal being, a being with all power, all knowledge, and all *goodness*. Moral progress therefore requires us to *update our idea of God*, much as we're continually updating computer software, and to think of God's goodness in a way that reflects our higher standards. Among other things, we have to start thinking of the idea of God as the idea of a being more relationally sensitive and less violent than the conventions of earlier times would have dictated. This is now what it takes to really have in mind the notion of perfect moral goodness.

The result is that atheism, the denial of God's existence, becomes easier to defend. The evolved God idea turns out to be subject to powerful new atheistic arguments which emerge as we notice how a personal deity good in the ways we now affirm should be expected to *recoil* from the thought of creating a world like ours. In short, as it evolves, the content of the God idea becomes simultaneously more admirable and less believable. This is theism's new evolutionary problem—a problem more bound up with cultural than with biological evolution.

My main point, then, is not that the world is outgrowing God, as one might initially be led to think on seeing atheism associated with progress. God is outgrowing the world! Less provocatively, the idea of God is ever more clearly finding a description too good to be true in our world. One of the ways this is happening is encapsulated by the new atheistic argument mentioned above—the hiddenness argument. What I develop in this book is, one might say, *the more general approach to the God debate hidden in the hiddenness argument*. In Chapter 6, I'll show how the hiddenness argument exemplifies it. But immediately afterward, in Chapters 7 and 8, I'll introduce a couple of different arguments that follow the same pattern.

It's the pattern that matters to me here, more than any individual argument. So those arguments in the book's second half are preceded by a discussion, in Chapters 4 and 5, of the neglected facts about moral evolution which give to the arguments their common life, which bubbles up from an updated understanding of the nature of a personal God. And before *that*, I want to get us more fully oriented for the book's discussions in Chapter 1 and also look, in Chapters 2 and 3, at certain ways of trying to reach atheism that have been influential recently, showing how they've been leading us astray and thus setting up the new approach.

This approach I call *progressive atheism*. I call it that not only because of the moral progress on which it draws but also because of the progress *for atheism* and *through atheism* that it may enable. Some important examples of the latter sorts of progress come into view when we work out how to apply the new approach in our cultural conversations. Both in relation to contemporary theistic philosophy more narrowly and in the culture at large, progressive atheism may prove consequential, leading us to new heights. This I try to show at the other end of the book, in Chapters 9 and 10. Such progress for and through atheism becomes possible, in part, because the new approach allows atheists to be positive about God instead of negative in ways that so often have led to bitter and pointlessly acrimonious disputes. Indeed, progressive atheism is *based* on a kind of positivity about God. Theists often say to one another, "Your God is too small!" But if I'm right, then theists should more and more be hearing this from atheists.

Growing all around.

1

Getting Oriented

This is a book on atheism. Questions about theism and atheism are philosophical questions. But not every book on atheism is a philosophical book. This one is. That's because it not only has a philosophical topic but is also committed to a philosophical approach. As we prepare to enter the hurly-burly province of human culture concerned with God, let's think about what that means and how it will matter. How will it affect our point of entry and the mode and directions of travel we choose? Since some of these choices might be queried, even by philosophers, I'll also be tackling this question: How can we show that these choices make sense? With answers to all these questions in hand, we'll be properly oriented and ready for our trip.

What philosophers want

Ludwig Wittgenstein was perhaps the most famous and certainly the most fascinating twentieth-century philosopher. Born into one of the wealthiest families of Europe, he gave away his inheritance and lived a life of austere simplicity, devoted to the intertwined goals of personal purity and philosophical clarity. Though deeply dissatisfied with the extent to which either goal was being achieved, and dogged by thoughts of suicide, his last recorded thought was nonetheless that he had had a wonderful life.

Wittgenstein's first great work, the *Tractatus Logico-Philosophicus*, was written while dodging bullets during the First World War. When the *Tractatus* started generating serious interest in his thinking, Wittgenstein agreed to cooperate with another Austrian, Friedrich Waismann, in the production of a book more fully explaining his thoughts. But poor Waismann had to keep starting over—the book was never finished. That's because Wittgenstein, true to his personal motto that one should always be willing to see one's problems as if for the first time, kept birthing new thoughts. A second great work, *Philosophical Investigations*, authored by Wittgenstein alone, did eventually emerge, but only after his death from cancer in 1951. In a 1999 issue of *Time* magazine on the Century's Greatest Minds, Daniel Dennett says of this work that it is "a model of thinking so intense, so pure, so self-critical that even its mistakes are gifts."

In Wittgenstein one sees the motives of the philosopher writ large. Philosophy addresses the most basic and difficult questions there are about life, the universe, and everything—questions such as what's ultimate in reality, how we can know about anything, what's the meaning and value of life, and what's the best way to live it. If you're philosophically minded, then you deeply desire to answer such questions. But you want to do it right. For you want *real* understanding, not some imposter. And you want it for its own sake, not just to impress yourself or others or to solve problems you're having with your relatives or to be happy. As the nineteenth-century British philosopher and social reformer John Stuart Mill wrote, expressing his preference for the philosophical life despite its agitations: "Better to be Socrates dissatisfied than the fool satisfied."

The first philosophers in the West, who wandered ancient Greece some 2,600 years ago, got their name because of this often-unsatisfied desire. Their attitude toward a difficult wisdom (*sophia*) deserved to be called love (*philia*). This love has a special quality that can at first seem paradoxical. It is a passion of indifference. The paradox is resolved by noting that the indifference is purely intellectual: if you've caught the philosophy bug, you want to know the truth, and the deepest truth, *regardless of what it may be.* A passionate indifference is needed to make you dig deep and to keep on digging without being distracted by biases or partisan interests or even by simple impatience, any one of which could have you quitting early. Of course, one also wants to see results, but philosophers are unusually restless and demanding, giving the most careful scrutiny to any alleged philosophical find and—in theory at least—quite willing to learn that discovered truths are still relatively elementary, a prelude to more digging.

Since their issues are too big and general to allow for the application of physical instruments, philosophers generally do their digging through careful reasoning alone, and early on they invented logic to help this reasoning along. Wittgenstein is sometimes described as a philosopher who *didn't* reason in the conventional way, who just sweated out refined jewels of insight. But in his case, I think it's more that another level of digging is needed: his writing is so terse and compressed that one has to dig to find the reasoning. Certainly many books have been written about Wittgenstein's reasoning. Individual examples of philosophical reasoning, of the movement from premises to conclusion, are called *arguments.* Such arguments, often quite intricately developed, play a role in philosophy comparable to the role of carefully designed experiments in science—to which the love of wisdom gave rise, partway through its journey from ancient Greece, for the sake of more specific and less fundamental questions about life and the universe. (Science, fortunately, has inherited philosophy's passionate indifference.) Arguments in philosophy allow us to test basic ideas and potentially even show them to be true, thus answering philosophical questions and giving philosophers what they want.

It's rather exciting when new arguments or ways of arguing are developed, much as it's exciting when someone designs a crucial experiment in science. Philosophers, like scientists, sometimes want to share this excitement and explain the general relevance and potential value of their work; that's how the world gets books like the one you hold in your hands. But the aim to achieve fundamental understanding must remain dominant. And a single breakthrough, while showing us where to dig, may also expose an urgent need for more breakthroughs.

God (and atheism) in philosophy

One important and basic idea philosophers have thought about, an idea at the heart of this book, is borrowed from religion. It's the idea that there is a *God*, a personal or person-like being who is all-powerful—and thus the creator of anything else, any world, there may be—and all-knowing, as well as perfectly morally good. The first two attributes mentioned here are commonly called omnipotence and omniscience. The third is sometimes called omnibenevolence, but that characterization, with its somewhat one-dimensional emphasis on doing good for others, doesn't really do the trick: think rather, and more generally, of a perfection of character and behavior.

A word we might be tempted to use in relation to God thus understood is "ultimate." We should yield to the temptation. If there were a God in this sense, it would be the ultimate reality. Otherwise put, then the ultimate reality would be personal. Though it's sometimes ignored, the ultimacy we've got here can be seen as having at least two dimensions (in Chapter 5 we'll see how a third might be added): God, if ultimate, is most fundamental in the nature of things, but may also be regarded as ultimate in inherent *value* or perfect. This overall perfection, more than moral perfection alone, is what the string of omni-attributes appears intended to signal. Many believers, and also many philosophers, at least implicitly think of God as ultimate in both ways.

When this idea of God is the conclusion of an argument, philosophers call the argument an argument for *theism*. Naturally, other philosophers have developed arguments for the denial of theism, the claim that there is no God. When this latter idea is the conclusion of an argument, philosophers call the argument an argument for *atheism*. Here you see one reason why in philosophy the atheist is not just someone who doesn't accept theism but, more strongly, someone who opposes it. (Another reason will emerge in a moment.) You also see a reason why in philosophy "atheism" tends to be taken as the denial of the *omni-God* idea rather than, more generally, as the denial of just any god or of all religious claims (more on this later too). If the argument for atheism is regarded as conclusive, philosophers easily switch in their talking from atheism-the-idea to atheism as a way of believing that has been justified. Generally, as when I speak of there being various roads to atheism, I will be using the term "atheism" in this second sense, to mean the way of believing that involves thinking God does not exist. I'll try to ensure that the context reliably indicates when that is not the case.

In some quarters there will likely still be concern about how I'm linking that term "atheism" to a denial of God's existence. Especially online, opinion seems to favor the idea that atheism is just the *absence* of belief in God. In this book, as I've made clear, I'll be assuming that atheism takes the further step to a claim of falsehood. This understanding, as we saw, grows out of philosophical practice. But there is another reason for accepting it, which will often apply even when atheism is being discussed outside philosophy. Most generally stated, it's this: although there are contexts, say, religious surveys, in which the other, broader, more permissive notion of atheism's attitude may be just the ticket, in contexts of inquiry about God that is not the case. Let me try to make this reason perfectly clear.

When I was in my early twenties, working at a summer job that had me in an employment agency trying to help others find summer jobs, I made a friend named Greg. Greg, I discovered to my surprise, had never thought about God. The subject had simply never come up. People who favor the broader notion of atheism do so because they think that people like Greg are "without God"—*atheos*—and so should be called atheists even though they haven't consciously rejected the idea of God as false. I don't want to debate the Greek roots of the term "atheist" here, so I'm happy to just concede that in some contexts, for some purposes, Greg might appropriately be called an atheist. But now suppose that Greg starts thinking about God, perhaps because I provoke him to do so. We start looking together at the *reasons* for affirming that God exists, and the reasons for denying this. We start doing some philosophy, engaging in philosophical *inquiry* about God. Greg doesn't become a theist. But he doesn't reject the theist's claim as false either. He neither holds that there is a God nor holds that there isn't but rather remains in a reflective state of doubt on the matter.

Believing that God exists, disbelieving this, and being in doubt about it are, once Greg starts thinking about God, the options available. So now, in this imagined context of inquiry, if we're going to say that anything weaker than a straight rejection of the idea of God as false can make Greg an atheist, we're going to have to say that being reflectively in doubt about these matters can do so. But we know that's not true. Why? Because at least since Charles Darwin's friend Thomas Huxley came up with the term, we've been calling someone in such a condition an *agnostic* rather than an atheist. In reflective, deliberative contexts, the space for atheism has shrunk because we've made room for that undecided position of agnosticism. Because in this book we'll be engaged in reflection and deliberation about God, it's accordingly appropriate for us to restrict the meaning of the term "atheist" so that it can properly be applied only to someone willing to take the position that theism is false.

Is the philosopher's God religiously irrelevant?

I've already started responding to those critical "queries" I mentioned at the beginning of this chapter. There are others. One other results from the fact that, in line with their interest in fundamental matters, philosophers who talk about God are usually *not* talking about the *Christian* God or the *Islamic* God or any other detailed form of theism—things generally don't get that specific. Rather, the focus is on the broader notion that all these specific ones have in common— their *root* notion, as it's sometimes called. This, once more, is just the idea of a personal being who is all-powerful, all-knowing, and perfectly good. You may wonder how such an abstract concern can be practically relevant. But it's highly relevant, since the more specific forms of theism—for example, the ones on display in churches each Sunday—depend on it. Without the root, there can be no tree. That is why it is wise for atheists to focus on the root idea of God. It's why I focus on it in this book. If only, say, some God whose attributes are supplied by a detailed reading of the Bible is shown not to exist, the result will not be nearly as profound or philosophically interesting. After all, even if *that* God doesn't exist, some other, shorn of some of those attributes, still might. But if the more fundamental claim of a generic theism is shown to be false, then no God exists. Philosophical atheists have good reason to be interested in so far-reaching a result as this.

But perhaps it will seem doubtful that the ultimistic notion on which I'm suggesting we concentrate is *really* at the heart of God-centered religious practice. Maybe philosophers focus on the idea of a person-like deity, and on the omni-deity, because it answers to their own concerns—for example, by providing one way of getting a fundamental explanation of why the world is as it is: God intentionally brings other things about, and *being* an omni-deity, being ultimate, represents the end of the line, explanatorily speaking. Indeed, maybe the personal omni-God is *only* the Philosopher's God, and not the God worshipped by ordinary believers. This sort of suggestion is fairly frequently made.

Let me explain as clearly as I can why I think the suggestion goes astray. The Philosopher's God, so-called, who has all power, all knowledge, and all goodness, is not some other God than, say, the Biblical God but rather represents *a collection of the same God's most basic features or attributes.* Philosophers pay attention to how religious believers behave, including what they say, and to the nature of their experiences, teasing out implications which believers themselves, who are often not all that interested in systematic understanding, may not have noticed. And these implications include the attributes on which philosophers focus.

Here the suggestion's reference to worship is actually quite illuminating, though not in a way that makes it more plausible. Worship in the strongest sense, commonly exemplified in God-centered religion, is an absolute and unqualified devotion. Thus, people generally don't in the religious manner *worship* something that they wouldn't on reflection regard as ultimate. In the personal case, this means *personally* ultimate, and leads directly to the thought that God must lack nothing in power, knowledge, and especially moral goodness. Moreover, the effect of religious experiences apparently of God, whether in contexts of worship or in some other context, is commonly to overwhelm and inspire awe in a manner that does not fit the notion of a finite and limited divine reality. Returning from such an experience, one cannot find *enough* superlatives to capture what one has encountered. It's not for nothing that in religious studies departments at our universities, the common search is for what this or that religious tradition regards as the ultimate reality—and in theistic traditions this is, again, a personal ultimate. It follows from these points that the philosopher's omni-God idea is not religiously irrelevant.

Now, it's easy to imagine that things are otherwise, that the religious idea you're encountering is not really an omni-idea or ultimistic, when you see people attributing to the divine qualities or sanctioning divine behavior you don't think very impressive or nice. An ultimate being would have to be better than that! But that *you* don't regard these attributes as impressive or nice, and so don't regard them as befitting ultimacy, doesn't mean that *they* don't view them thus (perhaps with the help of some excuse or unknown reason allegedly available to God that you would not credit). So believers can still be thinking of their God as unlimited and perfect, or be swiftly led to such thoughts with a bit of reflection, even if you would insist that they have fallen for a notion quite at odds with perfection.

Must a philosophical atheism have a broader conception of theism?

Some people would hold that it's for *philosophical* reasons, not because of a desire to be true to what's found in religion, that the idea of God should not be identified by atheists with the notion of an omni-God. They advocate other ways of thinking about God and conceptualizing theism that, so far, have proven less popular, and claim that one doesn't really have a basis for rejecting theism unless one can rule out all these other forms of the personal God idea too.

Take, for a particularly relevant example, the idea of process theism, which is deeply influenced by the thinking of the British philosopher Alfred North Whitehead. Whitehead's relations with his onetime friend and collaborator in an attempt to reduce mathematics to logic, the atheist Bertrand Russell, noticeably cooled when his (Whitehead's) distinctive metaphysical and religious interests became apparent. Whitehead's new work rested on the intriguing idea that the basic "things" of the world are *dynamic processes*, not static "beings." Change, time, and becoming are fundamental in the process view of reality. Now, you don't have to believe in any kind of God to be a process philosopher, though Whitehead did. But if you believe in God, you will conceive of God as more intimately related to the world, more bound up with processes of becoming, and thus more limited in certain respects than defenders of the omni-God idea could ever allow. God, on the process view, increases and changes with the world. Perhaps this sort of God could even be seen as progressing, morally, when we do. If so, it may be said, a swift move to another form of belief in God is available to anyone impressed by my arguments about moral progress in this book, even if the *omni*-God view should fall prey to them. And if *that's* so, then a powerful and significant atheism can hardly emerge from my arguments. To be powerful and significant, atheism must legitimize the rejection of all philosophical God ideas.

Let me explain why this philosophical objection should no more distract us from the course I'm setting, with my emphasis on the idea of a creative being with all power, all knowledge, and all goodness, than the religious one did before. I'll make the most obvious point first: the idea that a process theist might take God's goodness to be no greater than ours, growing as ours grows, is a nonstarter. Here it's illuminating to notice that when defending their view against the problem of evil, process theists emphasize their altered and attenuated understanding of God's *power*, not an altered view of God's goodness. They want their God to be worthy of worship too. Hence the arguments of this book may well enable a response to process theism and other personalist ideas of the divine as well as to the idea I'm making my focus.

Second, there are all kinds of ways in which a personal deity of some kind can be conceptualized, but for an idea to move to the center of philosophical discussion it helps if it is seen as doing serious philosophical work—for example, by providing fundamental explanations. And this, as suggested earlier, is how the idea of an ultimate omni-being has been seen in the history of philosophy. Since, as we saw in the previous section, this idea also has a special religious importance, indeed a central place in the history of Western religion, it's not hard to understand how "theism" has come to be associated with it and so "atheism" with its denial. Now, that's not to say that the idea should always dominate discussion of things theistic in philosophy. Not at all. Perhaps process theism or some other idea will at some point take its place. (There'll be more on this in Chapter 10.) But it does mean that *right now* the God idea involving omnipotence, omniscience, and perfect goodness has a uniquely important place in our culture. We're not done with it yet. Put the central point this way: there's some important *unfinished business* here, and a philosophical atheism may justly be preoccupied with it. In any event, my contribution in this book should be understood in relation to this unfinished business.

Shouldn't a philosophical atheism reject religious ideas of *every* kind?

This challenge invites a similar answer, though here we're moving in a somewhat different direction, thinking about the whole panoply of notions of the divine, including some that aren't personal and others that are even less worked out than the personal notions we've been discussing. Any reality that might be seen as divine, whether personal or not, would for some count as God. And many people think of atheists as denying that there is anything supernatural or transcendent or in any way beyond the reach of science, not just that there is a personal God. But to clarify to ourselves why a philosopher like me who thinks about religion—and indeed anyone who enters into the spirit of philosophy—might have a different view, it helps to remember what philosophers want.

When thinking philosophically we're not trying to advance some cultural agenda such as the agenda of those who defend science against its religious detractors and so would like to get rid of all things religious (here, as we'll see in the next chapter, is arguably where you find the famed "new atheists"). This isn't what philosophers want. We're simply trying to figure out what's true, without regard to what that may be. Or at least when we're doing our job this is our disposition. Now, a philosopher too might find attractive a really sweeping result: wouldn't it be interesting if we could just set aside all religious options! But desiring, as we've seen, *real* understanding and—like Wittgenstein—recognizing its difficulty, a philosopher will proceed cautiously in these precincts, naturally tackling this big goal in stages. (Special reasons for doing so at our stage of development will emerge in Chapter 3.) When it comes to God, the philosophical aim is best advanced by picking a fairly precise idea that would do some intellectual work for us were it true, and proceeding through very careful reasoning to determine whether it *is* true or instead false. This the idea of an ultimate personal God—a being with all power, all knowledge, and all goodness—supplies. Yes, other specific ideas might function similarly, but philosophers have for their own reasons long been preoccupied with the ultimate idea I've identified. We've seen that it's at the heart of most theistic religion too. As I put it before, there's some unfinished business here. And it's okay for philosophical atheism to associate itself with that unfinished business. It's okay to focus on *finishing* it!

When you think about it, there are in fact lots of ways—some represented in the world's religions and others at least imaginable— in which reality might include something that we come to regard as divine. The idea of an omni-God and indeed the whole collection of personal religious notions don't get us far down the list. We can leave open, when thinking about theism and atheism, whether some other idea from that list will turn out to be true if this one is false. We *should* leave that open. We shouldn't think, as many philosophers appear to do, that where the fundamental nature of reality is concerned, it's got to be God or nature: either there is a personal creator of some kind, or nature studied by science is all there is, the whole of reality. This is hardly passionate indifference. It takes neither the complexity of religion nor the difficulty of philosophy nor the immaturity of our philosophical efforts seriously.

Let me add a personal note. I've been viewed as an atheist ever since I proposed the hiddenness argument back in 1993 as an argument that might disprove the omni-God idea. That is not because I have kept referring to myself as an atheist, but because of views prevalent in philosophy and also online, where the hiddenness argument came to be discussed, about what behaviors are sufficient to warrant this designation. Even after it became clear that I deny *only* the omni-God idea and am open to other religious possibilities, I continued to be called an atheist. Now, if the challenges of this section and the previous one were sound, then none of this would be appropriate: I should never have been called an atheist, and indeed the appropriateness of the label in my case should always have been denied. So you get to choose. Either those challenges are wrongheaded or people have been wrong from the beginning to call me an atheist. I'm writing this book for those who would set aside the second option—even if only to see what things look like when our construal of what it is to be an atheist allows me to be one.

Can an atheist be *pro*-God?

In the next chapter, I'll be steering us away from a popular path to atheism that terminates in an error about the nature of God rather than in a justified belief that God does not exist. For those who are on this dead-end road, the belief that there is no God is combined with a negative evaluation of <u>the content of the God idea.</u> Atheists who have thoughts or feelings involving such a negative evaluation we can call *anti-God atheists.*

Now, the idea of God, in the form it takes in this book, is the idea of what would by definition have to be a rather *attractive* personal being—a being whose limitless power and knowledge are in the service of perfect goodness. So everyone who understands this idea of God should, in the relevant sense, be *pro*-God. This means it's an error to be anti-God instead. But I've found that some people have a hard time with the idea that even atheists can be—and should be— pro-God. So let me clarify what's at issue here. In particular, let me emphasize that being pro-God in my sense doesn't imply believing in God's existence, or hoping that God exists, or being soft on religion, or any other thing you might regard as being at odds with atheism, but only *giving to the content of the God idea a positive instead of a negative evaluation*. Lots of ideas that are clearly false or even impossible and could be misused by those who accept them nonetheless have a basic content that is good and deserves a positive evaluation. Take the idea of a kindly and ingenious species—call it Bod—that has managed, though only with enormous time and effort, to pulverize all the planet-threatening asteroids in the universe. This idea is false. You can imagine people getting all screwed up by believing it, maybe even making lots of trouble for the progress of science. But if you restrict your attention to the content of the idea itself, you'll have to give it a positive evaluation. What you're thinking about, when you hold the Bod idea before your mind, is really admirable and impressive. On reflection, and in my sense of "pro," we'll all be pro-Bod. Well, being pro-God, for an atheist, is like being pro-Bod.

Perhaps it will seem to some that my pro-God stance must have something to do with my endeavors on behalf of religion-after-atheism in other areas of my philosophical work, which I mentioned earlier in this chapter and also in the Preface. Positive there, positive here? But that is a mistake. The explanation is the one I just gave—an explanation that on reflection will compel assent for all those who *reject* my work in those other areas just as much as for those who warm to it. It is an explanation that I would continue to accept even if *I* came to reject all my other work—a result that, for a philosopher inspired by Wittgenstein, can never be ruled out.

2

An (A)Theological Dead End

In a third-season episode of TV's *The Big Bang Theory*, Penny wants Sheldon to teach her just enough physics to understand Leonard's work, and Sheldon, characteristically thorough, feels the need to start at the very beginning in ancient Greece: "It's a *warm* summer evening, circa 600 BC . . . ."

To find the origins of the older ways of defending atheism that our new way may supplant, we don't need to go quite that far back, but pretty close. The date mentioned by Sheldon marks the beginning of two hundred years of evenings that saw the work of a dozen or so significant thinkers, shadowy figures collectively known as the "Presocratics," a name that simultaneously insults them and compliments Socrates, the first ancient Greek philosopher most people have heard of. The Presocratics were no slouches themselves, coming up with some very interesting and influential ideas long before Socrates—or Plato or Aristotle, his intellectual descendants— emerged from the womb. Indeed, they began and pioneered both philosophy and science in the West (though science as we know it would arrive only many centuries later).

It's true that the Presocratics were more influenced by ancient Greek religious ideas than many—perhaps even including some of the Presocratics themselves—have thought. Moreover, happiness and the good life, not just understanding desired for its own sake, were commonly among the goals of their contemplation. But clearly they were also determined to apply close observation and reasoning when addressing big questions, and to make do without the mythological stories of the gods they'd grown up with, which they found reason didn't support. It's not hard to imagine how, restricting themselves in these ways, the Presocratics might have come up with little more than skepticism. They could have decided that human reason gives us no beliefs *more* reliable than religious beliefs. Or they could have proceeded cautiously, by not sticking their necks out when making claims about what was true or real, or by limiting the scope of their theories. But not many did. Perhaps this is understandable: they were experiencing an intoxicating rush of new ideas, and didn't have 2,600 years of similar work as a backdrop to their efforts. Some Presocratics, indeed, were exceedingly optimistic about reason's power, proposing bold alternative theories which they were apparently convinced told the whole story. Consider in particular the theory of the Atomists. According to this picture of things, reality consists of tiny atoms swirling in the endless void (what we would call empty space, still part of nature), in innumerable ways combining and falling apart, *and that's all.*

The Atomists—Leucippus, Democritus, and their followers, working in the fifth and fourth centuries BCE—not only came up with and developed an idea that, after long neglect and through various twists and turns, ultimately led to modern atomic theory. As my "and that's all" suggests, they were also among the first to develop an uncompromisingly nature-centered overall view of reality. They probably knew there were other options. Another Presocratic named Anaxagoras is said to have held a pluralist view according to which in addition to nature, which he like others saw as running on mechanistic principles, there is a transcendent mind. The Atomists in ancient Greece would have distinguished their picture of reality from such pluralist options. And just as their idea that matter is reducible into invisible particles has led to ideas influential in science today, so their view that nothing exists *apart* from atoms swirling in the void has generated a stream of thought flowing into the present. Those who swim in it today are called "metaphysical naturalists." As will become evident, the optimism of Atomistic thinking lives on in them.

Of course, science has come a long way since ancient Atomism and other early scientific ideas. Sheldon was preparing to tell Penny the long tale of how this went down in physics. The early Atomists, for example, thought of atoms as indivisible, but that idea was exploded in the twentieth century. However, what naturalists as such regard as true today is much the same as what, at the most general level, the Atomists too believed. Just like these ancient naturalists, they say that nature is all there is, and so hold that the kind of thinking and inquiry found in science, which has allowed us to penetrate nature in so many intriguing ways, is the only kind we will ever need to understand everything.

How pro-naturalism can lead to anti-God atheism

This view represents one way of getting on the road to atheism that in the previous chapter I called anti-God atheism, a road that, as noted there, amounts to a theological (or rather atheological) dead-end road, terminating in an error about the nature of God rather than in a justified belief that God does not exist. We'll be looking at a variety of ways of getting onto this road in the present chapter, many of them tempting in the context of current debates, and this naturalist way is the first one. I'm not saying that all naturalists make the mistake—many may not—or that naturalism itself is the problem. It's just tightly connected to a way of going there. To see how this works, let's think a bit more about what exactly naturalism is.

In philosophy the view is called *metaphysical* naturalism because it offers a picture of the fundamental nature of reality—or, at any rate, concrete reality (I'll leave aside such possible nonconcrete or abstract entities as numbers and sets). Metaphysics, as you may have guessed, is the part of philosophy concerned with basic issues about what's real. In the naturalistic picture, the world of nature is the only reality. Everything real belongs to a single system of natural law. Expand your thinking as far as you like beyond your bodily condition and conscious states and what's going on around you, beyond your home and the trees and mountains and sky and other planets and galaxies, beyond other universes and alien intelligences if there are any. You'll never encounter something real that doesn't belong to the same orderly if sometimes mysterious world to which we know all these things belong. Your conscious states belong to it too. So say the naturalists. Today's naturalists will usually add that this natural system is at least in principle fully open to scientific exploration. And that yields the naturalism–science link I've already identified. Indeed naturalists are typically very enthusiastic about science and about what it has shown of nature's regularities. Because science works with things that are clearly physical, it's generally assumed by naturalists, furthermore, that nature is a *physical* system, and this indeed is how you get the clear incompatibility between naturalism and the claim that God exists (a God would not be physical but the creator of anything physical there may be).

Now naturalism, when you think about it, offers quite an appealing picture of things. Everything—including us—is part of one complex web of nature, and scientists win heroism for unweaving it. Slowly, a few strands at a time, they are showing us why things work as they do. Naturalists are for this reason quite likely to be pro-naturalism and pro-science.

The attractiveness here itself has two strands, which are easily unwoven. First, the view held by naturalists will seem *intellectually* attractive. For example, it's theoretically extremely simple or uncomplicated—only one kind of thing exists. But second, it may affect the *emotions* of those who hold it, leading them to be drawn to this picture with a kind of affection. This will all the more be the case if naturalism is challenged, as it is in our culture by religion, and if it is challenged unworthily, as so often it is. Then fierce feelings of loyalty may be ignited.

What should we expect the religious results to be? The idea of God, as I've noted, is the idea of a being who is not part of nature but rather the creator of any natural universe there may be. So theism entails that nature is *not* the whole of reality and thus that naturalism is false. Would it be surprising, then, if by being pro-naturalism, and by seeing that naturalism is unworthily attacked from religious motives, some atheists who are also naturalists find their way into an anti-God disposition? Knowing what we all do of human nature, I don't think any of us will regard this as the least bit surprising. And given the complex social, emotional, and historical factors involved, what's going on here might be hard for those participating in it to see. So I suggest that one on-ramp to anti-God atheism is a susceptibility to certain emotional and intellectual effects of naturalism. Especially if believers in God are trying to undermine naturalism, and all the more so if they are doing it in ways that seem intellectually disreputable, someone who is pro-naturalism may become intellectually and also emotionally opposed to what these believers are talking about. And so she may become anti-God. Making God look bad may even be seen as a way of coming to the defense of naturalism.

Where this is going on, we see careful thought being sacrificed for the sake of activism—activism on behalf of naturalism. Moreover, if, due to pro-naturalism, someone is transferring to the opposition's belief in God the unworthy qualities they think attach to those who hold the belief, what we end up with amounts to little more than a crude ad hominem argument. After all, lots of nasty people have believed good things for bad reasons. Are we going to say that evolution's idea of the survival of the fittest is bad just because Hitler applied the idea in ways that fit his evil purposes? In the same way, we shouldn't say the idea of God is bad just because believers display some nastiness toward naturalism in its name.

But let's see whether there are any intellectually more serious thoughts here too. Might this be one? If naturalism is properly approved then the content of that other thing entailing its falsehood, namely theism, has to be *disapproved*. A few more serious thoughts and you should see the confusion. Contrary views like this can't both be true but they may both have content that, in the relevant intellectual sense, is good and worthy of approval. For example, according to physicists, general relativity and quantum mechanics can't both be right in their present forms, but the content of each is certainly interesting and would make of the alleged reality it describes something impressive, even beautiful. So that the content of theism should be disapproved doesn't follow from the correctness of pro-naturalism. It's a confusion to suppose otherwise. Now, a better argument might be available to pro-naturalism if theism postulated an *evil* God. But the relevant idea, defended as such in the previous chapter, is that of a perfect creator of any world there may be who has all power, all knowledge, and is morally all-good. If we try to think carefully and accurately and we consider the idea of God in its own right, not just in its connections to other things, we will see an impressive idea indeed. We can look at this idea and find plenty to admire in it even if we feel similarly about the idea of the naturalists.

The moral of the story? If you admire naturalism, beware of how this can mess up your thinking about God. Though a naturalism free of this vulnerability is also possible, naturalists would be wise to check for a pro-naturalistic anti-God atheism lurking among their beliefs.

Confusing God with the-World-plus-God

Some of the ways onto our (a)theological dead-end read are more subtle than others. The next one I want to discuss also originates in philosophy. It's a mistake that pro-naturalism might lead one to make, and so there is a connection to the previous section. But we don't need to assume that pro-naturalism is in play to see how it might be made.

The mistake is linked to something said by the well-known philosopher Thomas Nagel in one of his books. Theists have recently become very interested in it; Nagel's remarks have been cropping up all over the place. Here's what he said: "It isn't just that I don't believe in God and, naturally, hope that I'm right in my belief. It's that I hope there is no God! I don't want there to be a God; I don't want the universe to be like that." Nagel then goes on to speak of a "cosmic authority problem" lying behind his and—he conjectures—many other people's atheism.

This startlingly honest statement has been treated by some theists (some, not all) as clear and deliciously high-profile evidence for their view that the denial of God is owed not to careful investigation but to sinful self-assertion and resistance of God's demands. Never mind that a few lines further on Nagel says it would be silly to let one's hope

that there is no God influence one's investigation into whether there is
a God. This is a less juicy bit and rarely repeated. But after recognizing
the theistic opportunism manifested here, we may still see what Nagel
has said as problematic. For, in a couple of ways, it could easily be taken
in an anti-God direction. One way, the more obvious, involves Nagel's
fairly stereotyped view of God as a "cosmic authority." Bound up as it
is with patriarchal theistic religion, this view will be pertinent when
we address how God is easily confused with detailed *understandings*
of God generated by dispensable religious interpretations. The other
way is more subtle.

What Nagel's remark suggests is that it's possible to confuse how
we should feel about God per se with how we should feel about the
world in which we live with God suddenly, in imagination, *added*
to the picture. Call this combined phenomenon *The-World-plus-
God*. Here we need to remind ourselves that an atheist like Nagel,
unlike, say, your average Muslim or Christian, won't picture the world
as God-infused from the get-go. The world is the world. For many
atheists, who are naturalists, this means it is just one natural and
scientifically explorable thing after another, no matter how deeply or
widely you probe. In imagination adding God to *this* picture can be
jarring! For God has to be viewed as a very different sort of reality—a
nonnatural creator of nature, as we've noted. And there are various
ways in which this picture of two very different things stuck together
can appear unsettling and at least mildly distasteful to an atheist. A
simple pro-naturalism of the sort we were discussing in the previous
section might make it so. But it could happen in other ways too, which
involve more in the way of serious thought. For example (and here
I'm drawing on what a philosopher friend of mine recently said in a
talk), if we have to add God to the world, then it may seem that the
process of hard-won human learning and discovery loses its purity,
and that it has to come to a sudden end at some point—the latter

as we reach the stage where only revelation from someone perhaps reluctant to provide it could take us further, the former because *who knows* how many "extras" that can't be accounted for scientifically might have been introduced into the fabric of creation by its creator. On this view, certain impediments to human inquiry are the turnoff rather than any apparent affront to naturalism.

It's because something specific like this is experienced as a turnoff that thinking about The-World-plus-God can easily engender anti-God confusion. For distaste over The-World-plus-God thus produced can *illegitimately be transferred to God alone*. This is the confusion I have in mind. I don't know whether Nagel was led to think less highly of God just by thinking less than highly of The-World-plus-God; given his discriminatory powers, I suspect not. At least I hope not: I don't want the philosophical universe to be like that. But it seems quite plausible that some atheists may have fallen into this confusion. If so, we see here another way an anti-God position can arise, and for no good reason.

Why for no good reason? Because God, again, is to be understood as a perfect personal being with all power, all knowledge, and all goodness. That's it. And so God could be as awesome as you like even if The-World-plus-God would be disconcerting. (I'm not saying it would be.) Anyway, if The-World-plus-God really would, all things considered, be bad, then we shouldn't imagine God creating the world. In fact, then we'd have another reason to be atheists since, after all, the world exists.

Confusing theism with detailed *elaborations* of theism

Atheists are often suspected by believers of hating God. The so-called new atheists seem to delight in confirming this suspicion. Their leader,

Richard Dawkins, probably holds the record for the most provocative expression of anti-God atheism. He famously describes the God of the first 70 percent of the Bible as "jealous and proud of it; a petty, unjust, unforgiving control-freak; a vindictive, bloodthirsty ethnic cleanser; a misogynistic, homophobic, racist, infanticidal, genocidal, filicidal, pestilential, megalomaniacal, sadomasochistic, capriciously malevolent bully."

Okay! Not a pretty picture. As you'll note by leafing through his works, Dawkins sometimes upgrades God to a status of moral neutrality but rarely takes on the full candidate for ultimacy central to philosophical discussions of theism and atheism. And many of his followers are quite disinclined to distinguish between the nasty character he describes and God. This way lies confusion. For a being like the one Dawkins is thinking of here is an imposter. Even if you prove that this being doesn't exist, the *real* God still could. So why would new atheists waste their time in this way? The answer may be that they aren't wasting their time—given their actual aims. Although Dawkins and the other new atheists present themselves as defending clearheaded thinking about religious matters, none of these people, however clearheaded, is behaving like a thinker—at least not on religious matters. They are behaving like antireligious activists, who aim, among other things, to defend science against the antiscientific tendencies embedded in much conservative religion. And in that struggle, the conservative God would be the only God that matters.

Whatever the truth here may be (motives can be complex), my own aim at this point is just to defend the view that the sort of anti-God atheism we see here has to be set aside as confused when it is treated as an intellectually serious option and not an activist's strategy. The issue is the same one I alluded to in connection with Nagel, when I said there was another direction we could take from his remarks which would focus on his picture of God as a cosmic controller. There's nothing wrong with trying to get a more fine-grained conception of the nature of God; I'll be doing it myself in later chapters. But the idea of God, as such, is not to be identified with any such elaborated version. So even if some elaboration makes God look bad, the fault is with the elaborator, not with the idea.

In any case, what we're dealing with here is not really the result of intellectual reflection on the nature of God but rather what some believers in religious traditions such as Judaism, Christianity, and Islam have come to believe about God on the basis of apparent revelations of God's words and deeds. These are often "received" in circumstances in which the influence of fallible human authorities looms large. Now, it's easy to be influenced by such popular religious characterizations of God. God, if certain believers are to be believed, tells people to value "believing without seeing," lures them on with promises of paradise and seventy virgins, and smites people left and right who get in the way of "His" projects. However, what we see in such characterizations are not features of theism but rather features of some of the *specific forms of theism* found among the theistic religions of the world. And it's a mistake to confuse theism with them. Nothing in the idea of a creator of any world there may be, a perfect being with all power, all knowledge, and all goodness, leads you to the notion that God would be mean-spirited or want believers to follow God from unexamined self-interested motives or to believe without evidence. Quite the opposite. Nor for that matter—and here I return to Nagel's own interpretation—does it lead to the notion of a cosmic authority, a nosy despot who's always telling us what to do. These things follow instead from detailed versions of Christianity and Islam that not even all Christians or all Muslims accept. And atheism, as such, is not the denial of these detailed versions of Christianity and Islam.

True, as we saw in the last chapter, the denial of these versions of theism *follows* from what atheists hold, since a God of type X can't exist if *no God of any kind* exists. But it's not what atheism *is*. Here we have a really important distinction. Let me do a little more to make it perfectly clear. If atheism just were the denial of those detailed claims, then atheists could not also be committed to denying more moderate or less detailed versions of theism, as manifestly they are. How can their commitment be more thoroughgoing in this way? How can it be a rejection of theism and not just of *Christian* theism or *Islamic* theism or *Jewish* theism? Here's how. By virtue of the fact that it is a denial of the claim that there is a creator of any world there may be, a perfect being with all power, all knowledge, and all goodness! This is the more fundamental theistic claim to look to if you want to understand the meaning of "God" as opposed to "the Christian God" or "the Islamic God," or "the Jewish God." If this claim is false, then all the others are false too. (And that is why atheists will say they are false.) Sure, people who hold that fundamental claim to be true usually also hold many other claims about God to be true. And so it's easy to get caught up in discussion of these elaborations. But even if these elaborations entail the fundamental claim, it doesn't, logically, go the other way. Muslims and Jews and Christians and other theists have no monopoly on God. The fundamental claim, which defines the character of God and which atheism denies, does not entail the elaborations they have added. And so even if the brush used to produce the elaborations is applying horribly ugly paint, that's no reason to paint theism itself with the same brush.

God and the actual universe: A confusion of misdefinition

One way of making God as bad as you might think "He" would have to be on the basis of what some believers say is enabled by another mistake: supposing that it's part of the very definition of "God" that God has *created our universe* and is responsible for everything in it. Since creating a universe like ours, with all its suffering, is furthermore easily thought to be a very bad idea, the attitude toward God that results can easily be a negative one. This is a mistake I think we can avoid attributing to Nagel. But other seemingly serious thinkers have made it.

An example is found in the writing of Richard Carrier:

> The sort of God who would allow the things that happen in this world, must necessarily be the most horrible person imaginable.... That is why atheists say God is a horrible person. . . . That horrid God is the only kind of God compatible with the evidence; and surely no one, not even the Christian, should wish such a God would exist, nor praise it. . . . The God atheists are against is . . . the God that must necessarily exist, if any god does and the evidence is as it undeniably is.

Notice what Carrier doesn't say. He doesn't say that God, being perfectly good, would not allow the things that happen in our world, and so doesn't exist. No, he says that God is to be understood as the being *who allows these things*, and so Carrier has implicitly put God's creation of our world into his definition of "God." This generates a very unusual version of the problem of evil. Carrier's sort of atheist can't say that a God wouldn't permit evils, concluding that God doesn't exist because of the evils the world contains, as atheists traditionally have done. For it's part of the very idea of God that God allows these bad things to happen! The most Carrier's sort of atheist can do is rail against the idea that there should be a God—shaking his fist at the idea and announcing how very much he's *anti*-God, as Carrier in fact does.

I have no doubt that Carrier's heart is in the right place, but at least on this occasion his thinking has gone awry. For it is not, and

RV (

has never been, part of the very definition of theism that God creates our universe. But, you say, God isn't just any old omni-being; God is supposed to be the ultimate reality. Doesn't that make God, by definition, creator of the world? If you mean *our* world, the universe or universes that actually exist, then no, it doesn't. What it means is only that if God exists and there is a world, then the world's existence depends on the existence of God. (Notice that the world might be thus dependent even if infinitely old. Notice also that our understanding of "create" should therefore be broad enough to accommodate the idea of a world that has always existed: creation should not be taken as *entailing* origination.) We have to give God some freedom here. A God might see fit not to create any world at all: certainly the philosophical discussion of God has never defined this possibility away. Apart from some moments of carelessness, philosophers have always introduced into the definition of "God" only that God is the creator of any world there may be—this follows rather quickly from omnipotence and needn't even be mentioned in a definition of "God." Now, if you're a theologian, you have in addition to the definition of "God" the following premises to go on: "there is a world" (a no-brainer) and (most pertinently) "God exists." Theology by its very nature, as an effort of self-understanding on the part of a religious community, enjoys certain intellectual luxuries, including the luxury of assuming that God really exists. From all of this taken together, it can be deduced that God is the creator of a world and indeed of our world. But, as you can see, even theology doesn't get this information from the definition of "God" alone.

So—here's the result of our latest detective work—anti-God atheists should check whether their antipathy toward the God idea stems from mistakenly slipping into it a reference to our world and responsibility for all its imperfections. A natural mistake, perhaps. One easy to make. But still a mistake.

A confusion generated by the atheist's former beliefs

As we've been learning, there are various ways of getting on, or staying on, the dead-end road of anti-God atheism. So far we've noted four. We've seen how the anti-God attitude can illegitimately come from pro-naturalism, or from the transfer to God alone of the negative thoughts or feelings inspired by The-World-plus-God, or from conflating the basic idea of God with objectionable theistic details, or from slipping the creation of our world and responsibility for its imperfections into the very definition of "God." The fifth and final confusion to be considered once again involves theistic beliefs, but this time they're the former beliefs of the anti-God atheist herself.

Some atheists who confuse theism with detailed versions of theism have never themselves believed in God. They're in the position of John Stuart Mill, who said that unlike just about every other nonbeliever he knew, he had "not thrown off religious belief, but never had it." However quite a few of those who confuse theism with detailed versions of theism did once believe those very theistic ideas to be true. And so the detailed version of theism they have in mind may be the one they once accepted. If, perhaps not quite consciously, they are ashamed or disappointed in themselves for ever having done so and for their former naiveté, they may now be led, even in the midst of attempts at serious thought, to recoil at the thought of God. They find the anti-God approach attractive and maybe even become more susceptible to some of the errors diagnosed above because of the negativity that surrounds the fact that they ever naively, ignobly, believed as they once did. They have a negative attitude toward God derived from their negative attitude toward their former belief in God.

Such thinking is pretty clearly problematic and confused. There may be social and emotional factors that make a certain associated form of reasoning seem natural: for example, it was immature to believe in God, so God must be the sort of thing that only immature people would find appealing. But this reasoning, as anyone can see in a cool hour, is fallacious. For the kinds of thing that cause someone to believe in God, even if they include the thoughtlessness of youth or not seeing through self-proclaimed authority, have nothing to do with *God's* character. Even if it reflects very badly on you that you used to believe in God, it would be a mistake to take this out on God. It's really not a matter of such cosmic significance.

Of course, I'm not saying that every instance of anti-God atheism or its present popularity reflects all the problems we've uncovered in this chapter. One might be enough to lead you into the anti-God attitude and keep you there. If the various moves we've documented are various on-ramps taking you to this dead-end road, then some anti-God atheists use one on-ramp, some another. Some talk to travelers who got on elsewhere, adding to their reasons for staying on this road. Many, recently, have been talking to the new atheists. All are prevented from reaching a fully justified atheism.

So anti-God atheists should consider whether they've been misled in any of the ways we've gone through. That they have *somehow* been misled—at least if they continue to say it's God plain and simple that they intend to be talking about—is clear. As we've repeatedly noticed, simple reflection on the general idea of God will tell you so. In a pretty obvious sense, we should all be pro-God. But it may still be hard to hear what this idea has to tell us if complex cultural factors intrude. In part for this reason, it's easy to see the influence of naturalism as the most fundamental among the various sources of error we've considered. As we've seen, it represents a way of being an atheist that has deep roots in the West, roots trailing all the way back to ancient Greece. And it's not hard to see how someone affected by naturalism in the ways we've discussed might in a peculiarly naturalist fashion associate God negatively with the The-World-plus-God and—especially given how naturalism is related to science—be susceptible to a disparagement of believers and detailed theistic views that rubs off on God. Another reason to think naturalism of special importance here is that for many contemporary atheists, there's hardly any daylight at all between naturalism and atheism: the two positions, even if recognized as distinct, comingle to such an extent that their effects are joined.

It may therefore be tempting to think of naturalism as the main culprit in the ill-conceived attempt to use anti-God thinking in atheistic inquiry. But *precisely because of its cultural depth*, advocates of naturalism may wish to purify it of such error, avoiding any anti-God suggestions, and then put it to work on behalf of atheism's defense in a new way. It would be interesting if this worked out. Let's see if it does.

3

Naturalism's Shortcut

Can we solve the problems exposed in Chapter 2 by simply backing out of the dead-end road of anti-God atheism and charging onto this other road to atheism called naturalism? As we imagine the gravel rattling and prepare to give this possibility its due, let's get a bit clearer about some of the relations between atheism and naturalism.

Even those who recommend such a move will probably see that you don't have to be a naturalist to be an atheist. It's not as though inviting atheists onto the naturalistic road is showing them the way home. Atheists make a purely negative claim—but do note this is not the kind of negativity we were talking about in the last chapter!—which says that something is *not* the case, there is no God, not that something *is* the case, that nature is all there is. Moreover, their negative claim can be true in all kinds of possible scenarios, including ones in which the naturalist's claim is false. Suppose, for example, that some religious idea from Buddhism or from monistic forms of Hinduism or from Taoism turned out to be right. We aren't talking about anything like a personal God when describing the Buddha-nature, the monist's idea of Brahman, or the Tao. Instead, these ideas *compete* with the personal God idea, requiring the atheist's claim to be true. (The historical Buddha himself, Siddhartha Gautama, is often said to have seen this, and is just as often called an atheist.) But at least on the usual and relevant construals, the Buddha-nature, Brahman, and the Tao are pretty obviously not natural entities, open to the examination of science. They require nature to be less than all there is just as much as theism does. So if a nontheistic religious idea of this sort turned out to be right, the atheist's claim would be true but the naturalist's would be false. It follows that an atheist is not, just as such, rationally committed to naturalism. Rather, by signing on for naturalism, the atheist *adds* something to her denial of the existence of God—and rather a lot.

Having said all that, naturalism still is closely related to atheism in another way. It's not just a position one might happen to take while also being an atheist. Even if you don't have to be a naturalist to be an atheist, you do have to be an atheist to be a naturalist. That's because if the Atomists are correct in thinking that reality is atoms in the void and that's all, then Anaxagoras can't be right in postulating Mind. If nature is all there is, then there can't also be a God who transcends nature. Any naturalist, therefore, who considers what she's intellectually committed to by reason of her naturalism will pretty quickly see that she's committed to atheism.

This point has an interesting consequence: *any good reason to believe naturalism will immediately justify atheism too.* A defense of naturalistic belief, in other words, can do double duty as a defense of atheistic belief. Might this sort of move be made successful? Does naturalism, disentangled from anti-God associations, offer a straight and smooth and swift transition to a justified atheism? Or is it instead a questionable shortcut?

Naturalism's simplicity argument, and some unsuccessful replies

One of the biggest things naturalism has going for it is its simplicity. I mean this in the sense of economy: a view about the nature of reality is simple, in this sense, to the extent that it can avoid referring to many things or many kinds of thing. Reality, on the naturalistic view, is in one way as simple as can be: only *a single* kind of thing exists, namely, natural stuff—stuff that conforms to what we call "laws of nature," which make of nature and so of reality the unified system that naturalists believe it to be. Nature is, of course, still nonsimple or complex in another respect: there are lots and lots of *things*, as well as connections among things, codified in those laws of nature. But this is a complexity that every credible picture of reality will have to accommodate. And so the naturalist can claim to be ahead of the game by making no additional division between nature and supernature, with the latter a perhaps incomprehensibly different kind of thing.

This simplicity in the naturalist view is connected to some reasoning that can be developed to support accepting the view as true. Naturalists have shown a taste for such reasoning. We should try to expose it as clearly and forcefully as possible. Here goes.

Science is, at the very least, a really impressive human intellectual achievement, and, as it expands, science brings ever more of what we experience into a single natural system. This includes our most profound experiences of apparently religious objects that seem to "transcend" nature. (Science has at any rate made a good start on doing so in the cognitive science of religion.) That is just how we should expect it to be, given that science clearly shows how we ourselves aren't somehow injected into the natural world from outside: we aren't born *into* the world but *from* the world, as part of a complex evolutionary process whose details are becoming ever clearer to us. There is indeed no explanatory need for anything over and above nature; the thought of such an alien dimension of reality—however appealing it may be to certain nonintellectual dimensions of our own reality—should from an intellectual point of view seem to us an odd extravagance. Just as we would look with incredulity or pity on someone who said that the operation of their watch might depend not only on its gears and spring but also on a couple of invisible gremlins inside the watch, who aid its movements from time to time, so we should look with incredulity or pity on someone who supposes that beyond nature might be supernature, with its own entities and powers, not subject to nature's laws and in some way deeper, more fundamental, than them.

I think we can learn a lot about naturalism and the issues it raises by examining this reasoning. But first let me explain why some reactions to this reasoning that would most likely be popular, especially among religious thinkers, are unsuccessful.

What we're likely to hear is that religion can explain things naturalism is *unable* to explain, such as the origin of life or the nature of consciousness or why there is something rather than nothing, and so the argument's claim that there is no explanatory need for anything over and above nature is false. But this is unconvincing. All we can reasonably claim is that naturalism has not *yet* found a way to deal adequately with the first two items mentioned here, the origin of life and the problem of consciousness. Thinking in terms of science's own timescales, we can see that human science and philosophy have just got started; and thinking in terms of biological evolution, about which we humans have recently learned a lot, we can see that adaptive needs and environments in the history of evolution on this planet might have been such as to give our cognitive capacities a peculiar *slant*, which enables us to solve certain problems easily but makes other problems quite difficult for us. And the difficult problems might very well include the two in question. Take the problem of consciousness in particular—the problem, roughly, of why all that the physical brain does should be accompanied by subjective experiential states, why there should be "something it is like from the inside" to be in this or that brain state. As the philosopher Colin McGinn suggests, beings in other worlds, differently evolved, might find the problem of consciousness a snap and labor to do physics or chemistry. For us, it's more like the other way around. In terms of what we've already come to know, then, it makes perfect sense for the naturalist to ask for more time in relation to the explanatory tasks in question: certainly it hasn't *yet* been shown that naturalism is "unable" to explain these things or that a non-naturalistic account of these things is "needed."

What about the third item: the problem of why there is something rather than nothing? Here the point seems to me a nonstarter because religion has no explanatory advantage over naturalism in this regard. It too has to live with this problem. Now, you may say that *God* exists necessarily in the strongest sense, and since such a necessary being has to exist—meaning it can't *not* exist—the question why there is something rather than nothing in this scenario just goes away. Religion provides a satisfactory explanation. Since God necessarily exists, there *can't* be nothing! But as the philosopher David Hume pointed out more than three hundred years ago, it's pretty hard to imagine just how it should be that God, a concrete being, simply has to exist: if we can think of a thing as existing, we can think of it as not existing too. Atheism may be false but it's not unthinkable! Being in the most abstract sense "able" not to exist seems the price any being pays for being a concrete thing. (Here concrete beings may be contrasted with abstract truths, such as the truth that 2 + 2 = 4, which does indeed seem necessary.) As Hume also slyly suggests, if despite these difficulties we want to say that God is a necessary being, we are handing the naturalist the perfect retort. For it's *no more* difficult to grasp how the existence of the *natural world*, in some configuration, could be necessary. And it's simpler, to boot, to say that it alone exists. So this has now become the preferable option—one that, as you may have noticed, brings with it just as good a solution to the problem of why there is something rather than nothing as we were offered by the theist. Indeed, it's really the same one!

A second, quite different sort of move that's likely to be tempting in reaction to the argument we're considering, though improperly so, says that even if naturalism can explain religious experiences, it doesn't follow that they're delusory. Consider your dog Banjo. Maybe a clever neuroscientist could, with a brain probe, reliably produce Banjo hallucinations for you and also show where in your brain such hallucinations can be triggered without her help. This shouldn't make you any less ready to believe the testimony of your senses when it appears to you that you have come through the door and Banjo is slobbering all over you. Indeed, we all think ordinary sensory experience often conveys truths despite what we know about the natural capacities of the brain—not to mention about neuroscientists and brain probes.

This is all very well, a defender of the naturalist argument can reply, but the reaction misses the point. The point is not that apparent perceptions should be rejected as misleading whenever we can explain them without supposing that they're putting us in touch with reality, but rather that if we can account for them in natural terms alone, it would be odd and faintly ridiculous to think we need a whole extra dimension of reality to do the job. The thing to notice about Banjo is that we can accept his existence and, more generally, the reliability of sensory experience *without ever leaving the natural realm*. We couldn't do the same for religious entities and religious experiences.

A better response?

The critical responses to our naturalistic argument surveyed so far look weak. Is there a better response, or does the naturalistic argument go through successfully and naturalism with it? I think there is a better response, which shows that the naturalistic argument doesn't work. By the same token, it will show that naturalism itself, if not provably false, is nonetheless highly questionable.

Consider again the suggestion of one of the responses we tested earlier, according to which the naturalistic argument's claim that there is no explanatory need for anything over and above nature is *false*. This claim is hard to defend in its original form, but it is quite plausible in a weakened form, and in that form it still puts the argument out of commission. What we should say is that although the naturalistic argument's claim that there is no explanatory need for anything over and above nature may not be clearly false, there is still good reason to be in *doubt* about it and so not to believe it. And if *that's* true, if we should be in doubt about whether anything over and above nature exists, then pretty clearly there's good reason to be in doubt about—and so not to believe—naturalism.

The relevant reason to be in doubt can be found in naturalism's simplicity argument itself. All any such argument can say about science's power is what this one does say—that science is bringing ever more of *what we experience* into the natural realm. Might it not be that what humans so far have had access to through their experience doesn't reflect what there *is* in the way needed for the naturalistic argument to be right in its claim, which is, after all, completely comprehensive? Might we have missed vital aspects of reality that fit more awkwardly, if at all, into science's picture? In particular, might our experience offer too small a sample to generate adequate support for naturalism's explanatory confidence?

Yes, yes, and yes. Here a couple of points I used before to defend naturalism become relevant again, though this time by making trouble for it instead. I said that, thinking in terms of science's own timescales, we can see that human science and philosophy have just got started. Many new and important discoveries may lie in the future, and we should adjust for this in our reasoning. But this helps to make questionable the idea that our sample of experience is big enough to make it trustworthy when called in support of naturalism. Perhaps some of those future discoveries will come as a result of *religion* pulling up its socks. Earlier I also said that, thinking in terms of biological evolution, our cognitive capacities might have received a peculiar slant conducive to certain kinds of problem-solving but unfavorable to others. This suggests that, regardless of the issue of sample size, our experience may, as it were, be *biased* in favor of certain kinds of reality—the kind that science, the crown jewel of human intellectual effort so far, is able to process.

And now we can also see why there's a problem with the tempting analogy I put into the naturalistic argument. Here it is again. Just as we would look with incredulity or pity on someone who said that the operation of their watch might depend not only on its gears and spring but also on a couple of invisible gremlins inside the watch, who aid its movements from time to time, so we should look with incredulity or pity on someone who supposes that beyond nature might be supernature, with its own entities and powers, not subject to nature's laws and in some way deeper, more fundamental, than them.

What's the right answer to this reasoning? Now it may not be hard to see. An analogy argument like this works only if the reason we should say the *first* thing is a reason to say the *second* as well. So why should we look with incredulity or pity on the gremlin claim in relation to the watch? Because *we* know all about watches, having created them ourselves, and gremlins have no part in their processes. Here our experience is enough. But we can't be confident in the same way that we know all about nature as a whole and about the causes of all its processes. And so it doesn't follow that we should look *in the same way* on those who respond to naturalism with supernaturalism.

Of course, naturalism might still be correct and supernaturalism false. The point is just that *this* reasoning doesn't establish these things, and it doesn't do so despite naturalism's relative simplicity. Furthermore, what prevents it from doing so—the uneliminated possibility that nature as a whole is in some way, perhaps one we have no clue about, dynamically related to realities beyond it—also prevents us from legitimately believing naturalism to be true. And thus we are prevented from charging the short further distance to atheism, using the naturalistic shortcut.

Going macro on maturity

The previous section gives us a sense of why no one should depend on the naturalistic shortcut to atheism. In the remainder of this chapter I want to strengthen and deepen this sense by adding some detail, filling out a bit the outline of reasoning I've provided. I'll focus on one of the ideas I've been emphasizing because it has been neglected in inquiry about naturalism. And I'll put the idea this way. The naturalistic shortcut is questionable because it is questionable whether human inquiry is *mature* enough to allow us to know what the naturalist claims to know.

Earlier I suggested this point about questionable maturity in connection with the "big picture" science offers us, which becomes dramatically evident when one starts to appreciate the immensities of time casually accommodated by scientific timescales. Let's start by thinking a bit more about that big picture. To see it, one has to shift from what we might call the small-scale or *micro* level of individual human lives and communities and their intellectual activities to the large scale or *macro* level, zooming out to the point where all our intellectual doings appear together with all our other doings in their broader natural context. At this macro level, where the consequences of deep geological time and planetary evolutionary processes become visible, we'll see human truth-seekers as belonging to one species of animal among others, evolving over hundreds of thousands of years, slowly spreading around the globe, but with potentially many thousands—even hundreds of thousands—of years remaining in which to do plenty of new things. Stunningly, according to science, even another 200,000 years, which is a hundred times as long as the period separating you from Jesus of Nazareth, would take our species only about halfway to the average lifespan of mammal species on our planet.

So where does *thinking* about the world, human inquiry, fit in this big picture? If what we have in mind is explicitly organized, persistent, systematic human inquiry, we need to go back in time no more than a few thousand years to cover the period that holds all of it. From our present vantage point, that must strike us as an incredibly short period. With a bit of luck, this few thousand years could easily be turned into tens of thousands or even hundreds of thousands of years. Furthermore, if we're thinking of systematic inquiry, we should observe that according to science, we're the first species on our planet to mull over intellectual problems in this way. How many other species—whether organic or nonorganic—will follow in the billion years that, we are told, remain for life on Earth, and what will they learn?

A strong sense of intellectual immaturity may come with careful reflection on such considerations. At 300,000 years or so of age, we're still a young mammal species, and given that only the last few thousand years from that period have involved organized systematic inquiry, it may appear that we've just got started on a disciplined intellectual exploration of the world. Sure, we've discovered a lot, but a great deal more may be waiting for us—or for those who follow us—around distant corners. However, we should be careful here. It's at least conceivable that we're at a late and advanced stage *developmentally* even though *temporally* at an early one. So what should we say? Is this the case? Are we intellectually developed beyond our years? Is the species a child prodigy? Or is there reason to question this notion—reason to wonder whether our species might be rather less than developmentally mature where matters of the intellect are concerned?

To see that we ought to go with door number two, it will help to get a bit clearer about the notions of development and intellectual maturity we've started to deploy. In speaking of development, I am, of course, pushing us some distance beyond the uses of the term one finds in science—say, in evolutionary developmental biology or in developmental psychology. But that needn't be a problem. It makes sense to speak of development for human beings or their endeavors, and also of maturity and immaturity, whenever we can mark our position on a scale relative to something counting as the attainment of some relevant commodity, and whenever we can move further from or closer to this attainment. For our purposes, we can use an understanding of intellectual development at the macro level that is structured by the notion of intellectual *goals*—and in particular by the goal of a deep and wide understanding of the nature of reality. This will make our approach directly relevant to the aspirations of naturalism. Human inquiry, for us, will be judged intellectually mature or immature, developed or undeveloped, by reference to how closely this goal has been approached.

Now, our ordinary ways of talking about immaturity suggest that an important distinction should be taken into account before we go any further. Suppose someone at the everyday micro level calls you immature in relation to the intellectual life. They're obviously suggesting that you're in some way undeveloped. But the sense in which that's so depends on whether they're looking into the past, noticing your *shortcomings*, or looking into the future, acknowledging your *potential*. Think of someone who's been goofing off in the early years of school, getting less done than might reasonably have been expected. Such an individual shows immaturity in the first sense. But in terms of high school attainments even the hardest-working student who's just entered grade 1 displays immaturity in the second sense. She's just started down the road to grade 12, and so hasn't got nearly as far as eventually she will, if she lives on and keeps plugging away. And the two sorts of immaturity, immaturity-as-shortcoming and immaturity-as-potential, can be connected in various ways. One might, for example, need to get rid of the former to retain the latter. At a certain point, if you keep goofing off, you may have put the kibosh on your potential for serious secondary school advancements.

Let's now take this distinction between immaturity-as-shortcoming and immaturity-as-potential from the micro to the macro level, remembering what we've already said about development toward the larger intellectual goal. Whether it's easy to discern or not, human intellectual life at that level might display either sort of immaturity, leaving our species at an early stage, intellectually speaking, both temporally *and developmentally*. We could have made enough bad intellectual—or intellectually relevant—moves or acquired enough intellectual liabilities in our brief past to keep us quite undeveloped, intellectually speaking, in relation to the broadest goal of human intellectual life. This would be immaturity-as-shortcoming. And immaturity-as-potential? That could represent our condition even if our past intellectual behavior were in every way excellent, because of, for example, the severe difficulty of achieving our goal. Thus our maturity would be questionable if we had evidence of relevant shortcomings or of being yet some distance from our goal or of both—perhaps with signs that the former condition had something to do with the latter. Do we?

The maturity problem

As it happens, we have all these things. Our maturity in relation to the goal of a deep and wide understanding of reality is seriously questionable. For evidence of relevant shortcomings, consider sexism across the ages: neglectful of women's actual and possible contributions, we've not yet even managed to bring all available human resources to bear on our intellectual problems. This may very well have produced developmental delays, if only because we've not had as many creative minds hard at work as we would otherwise have had.

Consider also how often our intellectual work has been corrupted by ideology. For example, evolution is still often resisted on religious grounds, and for centuries in Europe cultural support for belief in intelligent design kept religious explanations central where evolutionary thought might otherwise have been developed and reached something like its present condition.

And then there are cognitive biases and heuristics, unconscious errors of reasoning or potentially misleading mental shortcuts affecting us all, such as the famous confirmation bias and in-group bias. Only recently acquired, our familiarity with these cognitive quirks continues to grow and deepen as we continue to notice and distinguish ways in which misleading information-processing behaviors seem to have become adaptive for *Homo* species in the history of evolution. Time-consuming workarounds—such as the double-blind experiment—have had to be developed to deal with them.

Dozens of examples of biases and heuristics have been found by means of ingenious experiments, such as those exposing what is called "anchoring," the tendency to be affected in numerical judgments by the numbers, high or low, to which you've recently and irrelevantly been exposed. In one such experiment, experienced judges were inclined to give a shoplifter a longer sentence if a higher number had just come up when they rolled a pair of dice. The psychologists Daniel Kahneman and Amos Tversky are responsible for waking us up to such irrational tendencies, and they have emphasized how difficult they can be to avoid. Amusingly, the reviewer of a Kahneman essay collection in 1984 was able to point out that the process by which its papers were selected betrayed three of them: anchoring, availability, and representativeness!

When we are inclined to boast about how much humans have accomplished in inquiry over the past few thousand years, we need to remember all these "impurities" in evolved human intellectual behavior, and also the various ways they must surely interact. There is evidence, for example, that ideology and prejudice are sometimes causally linked to cognitive biases. If we could see the joint influence of these things on our intellectual conversations across the centuries as we see genetic structures, we might notice long stretches of "junk" intellectual DNA. Of course, for some of these things, we're obviously not blameworthy in quite the same way someone might be blameworthy for goofing off at school, but where they have held us back and prevented us from developing, intellectually, as otherwise we could have done, we still have an immaturity of the first kind, associated with shortcomings.

How about evidence that we are still some distance from the goal of a deep and wide understanding of reality? For immaturity-as-potential at the macro level? We can think about this without worrying about the influence of shortcomings like those we've just been talking about. Even if you think none of them is worrisome, you'll be able to see how science's maturity in the sense of its attainment (or near attainment) of the goal of a deep and wide understanding of reality is open to question. By discovering certain powerful methods, and unifying a lot of us around them, science has figured out how to get our movements related to the larger physical environment in ways yielding information about it—information we can use to rocket off to the moon or just bring pleasure to our ever-curious prefrontal cortex. This is hugely impressive. But it can also be misleading. For even science has its frontiers—and no one knows how much territory lies beyond them. Science, so far, might have done little more than pluck the low-hanging fruit. Deep time and evolution, for example, are great. But what about a reconciliation of general relativity and quantum mechanics? Or a reconciliation of the natural and social sciences? Even if no longer in its infancy, science too may still be immature.

Biology, among other scientific areas, is not exempt. In his book *Behave: The Biology of Humans at Our Best and Worst*, Robert M. Sapolsky makes a point of emphasizing the many new links between biology and our social behaviors that have been discovered very recently. Most of the forces by which our behaviors are shaped, he says, "involve biology that, not that long ago, we didn't know existed." One wonders how much more information we'll have on such matters in another hundred years, or in a thousand.

And such information may also move us a lot further in philosophy's part of the quest for a deep and wide understanding of reality, which at the present stage often seems able to deliver little more than disagreement. One wonders what new support for positions (or new positions) on free will or on broader issues in social and political philosophy will be suggested by it. Similar questions are easily sparked about connections between metaphysics and future physics, between ethics and future work on cultural evolution, or between epistemology and the future of artificial intelligence. Perhaps the most noticeable area in philosophy where we're apparently a long way from the finish line is the philosophy of mind, which has bequeathed to us the difficult philosophical problem of consciousness—a rather big problem that naturalists themselves (as suggested a bit earlier on in this chapter) are forced to admit is unsolved.

Seeing all these ways in which our macro-level intellectual maturity, in the sense in which we've defined it, is indeed questionable, it will be hard to resist the further thought that our shortcomings may have had something to do with that fact. Indeed, we already saw some evidence of this when giving examples of those shortcomings earlier in this section. But we can now make the point more pointedly. For example: Would the reconciliation of the natural and social sciences be aided by the removal of sexism from inquiry? Would biology dart ahead given the final removal of cultural prejudices from our societies? Would philosophical disagreements be diminished by a fuller acknowledgment of our cognitive biases and the humility that—one may hope—would spring from that? It's hard to tell. But that the answers are all negative would be hard to sustain.

Is the maturity problem a problem for naturalism?

What we've been collecting are signs of human intellectual immaturity at the macro level, and we've seen enough evidence of it to say that maturity—the realization (or near realization) of a deep and wide understanding of reality—may yet be a long way off. *May* be: remember that all I aimed to show is the *questionableness* of our maturity. The next step is to see what all of this means for naturalism and the naturalistic shortcut to atheism.

It will perhaps be clear that there is a pretty important relationship between what naturalism claims and the aspiration of a deep and wide understanding of reality. If naturalistic belief were justified, then we could have a justified belief about the character of reality at the widest and deepest levels. So it looks as though the questionableness of our intellectual maturity, in the sense in which I have sought to display it, brings with it the questionableness of the idea that naturalistic belief has yet been justified for us. Here we see again—now with more detailed support—the point from the end of the previous section about "the uneliminated possibility that nature as a whole is in some way, perhaps one we have no clue about, dynamically related to realities beyond it."

How might the naturalist reply? One suggestion, which I would expect some naturalists to come up with fairly quickly, is that any inclination we have to resist or question naturalism is itself naturally explicable—and indeed a product of human immaturity! A thought experiment will be useful. Imagine that science in its modern form, with its hugely transformative power, had come first—*before* religion instead of the other way around. And imagine that science had, in that early incarnation, found ways of meeting everyone's material needs, which humans immediately implemented. Suppose, further, that human lifespans had been indefinitely extended by scientific discoveries so that no fear of dying ever arose. And now ask yourself this: If you were one of the people in this other world, would non-naturalistic ideas such as religious ideas get any kind of grip on you, intellectually? Would you still be inclined to resist or question naturalism? The thought here, one that naturalist writings often reveal, is that if we resist or question naturalism, it's entirely because of the influence on us of nonintellectual factors such as misery or dissatisfaction with our lot in life or a fear of death. The naturalist is likely to think of these as shortcomings, but all his argument really needs, of course, is that they be actual and operative in the manner described.

One quick response to this move would simply remind us of the religious experiences we were discussing earlier in this chapter. Even in a possible world like that imagined in the thought experiment, people might have religious experiences, and if they did, that would represent an additional and more intellectually relevant factor. The more basic problem with this response to our questioning of naturalism, however, is that our own discussion in these last few pages of the neglected issue of human immaturity is a clear counterexample to it: here *reasons* are given for finding naturalism questionable. If our motives are supplied by philosophy and our interest is in the truth, *whatever it might be*, these reasons should matter to us.

In our circumstances, a certain intellectual modesty seems called for. Remember our little thought experiment from the beginning of the previous chapter about how the beginning of ancient Greek philosophy might have been different? About how the optimism might have been dialed back and less comprehensive theories formulated? That's relevant here. Alternative rational approaches occupy the space between a radical skeptical unwillingness to grant reason any power, at the one extreme, and completely comprehensive rational accounts like that of the naturalistic Atomists, at the other, which try—at least in outline—to tell the whole story of reality. And so we have another possible past. It could have been that the first philosophers in the West discovered some really good arguments for this or that claim about the universe without committing themselves to any comprehensive theory such as that associated with naturalism, which is not just a negative claim that denies something but a positive one, the affirmation of a controversial picture of the overall shape of reality. There could even have been a non-naturalistic form of Atomism, which restricted itself to the behavior of material things, leaving open the question whether there's anything in reality that, unlike us, is not material in nature. Perhaps its intellectual influences would have been different and more in line with the openness demanded of a genuine truth-seeker, *especially* at the very beginning of systematic rational inquiry.

That's a very good criticism of the Atomists, a naturalist may reply, but today things are different. We've had 2,500 years of wide-ranging discussion in which science has gone from strength to strength and non-naturalistic options have wilted. So it doesn't matter that a naturalistic Atomism at the very beginning of the history of rational inquiry in the West was a tad presumptuous.

However, right here a new and peculiarly relevant form of immaturity-as-shortcoming rears its head and causes trouble for naturalism. Look closely at those 2,500 years. The main cultural discussions of religion in the West after the decline of Greek philosophy were focused on the theistic religion that largely took its place, namely Christianity. Its ideas were for hundreds of years treated as representing the only important—the only really live—religious options. And we are still influenced by this narrowness of vision from which our ancestors suffered. The religious and the irreligious alike often still behave as though Christianity is the only religious game in town. The Reverend Thwackum, a character in the Henry Fielding novel *Tom Jones*, remarks that "[when] I say religion, I mean the Christian religion, and when I say the Christian religion, I mean the Protestant religion, and when I say the Protestant religion, I mean the Church of England!" It would be an interesting exercise to check sometime how often when popular writers or even philosophers speak of religion they do so in the Thwackum way (though without his charming willingness to be up front about it), with an emotionally appealing but rationally illicit focus on some presently influential religion, together with the assumption that *religion contains no other important ideas*. Atheists too can betray the habit, meaning by religion "what used to be my religion" or "the form of religion I grew up with."

This spiritual ethnocentrism is, I suggest, one of the features of a continuing intellectual immaturity present among human beings. There are many other signs of it. Take the fact that secular religious studies departments are only now springing up in our universities. As their investigations make abundantly clear, the world has seen, and still offers today, many religious ideas inconsistent with naturalism other than Christian ideas. The Hindu, Taoist, and Buddhist ideas mentioned earlier are among them. With how many of these ideas are today's Western naturalists really well acquainted?

It's instructive, in this context, to note how relatively simplistic is your average naturalist's treatment of these other religious possibilities. They are commonly lumped under the label of the "supernatural" and associated with "spooky stuff"—talk of ghosts and other paranormal phenomena that have been scientifically debunked. This encourages the thought that religion is by its very nature at odds with science while at the same time taking our attention away from genuinely religious phenomena, which may have little to do with spooky stuff. The idea of the supernatural is also often read as telling us that there are two quite distinct departments of reality: a "lower" one of nature and on "top" of it supernature. This is at odds with at least some nontheistic religious ideas already found in the world, such as those of Advaita Vedanta in Hinduism, according to which nature is *part* of a larger reality, and may well be at odds with many new religious ideas of the future. Moreover, the notion of the supernatural as deployed by naturalists, though sometimes sensitive to wider studies of religion, especially ones with an evolutionary base, is nonetheless often biased in the direction of gods or godlike entities. This encourages the thought that, having dealt with God, the "highest" godlike religious reality, naturalism has nothing to fear from other religious ideas, which are, as it were, dim reflections of what God-centered religion is going on about. And that thought is at best highly premature, since if there are religious profundities that humans are presently in a very poor position to imagine, they will have little to do with gods but are also excluded by naturalism.

So what should someone say about naturalistic belief who fully recognizes the important results of scientific inquiry, if properly sensitive to all that we've seen of the questionableness of human intellectual immaturity and *also* the evidence of a distinctively religious brand of immaturity I've just put forward? I think she should say that things haven't changed much since the days of ancient Greece: the move from science to naturalistic belief remains a leap. For by believing naturalism we rule out all these other views that haven't even properly been discussed yet—the whole panoply of non-naturalistic possibilities. We dismiss such ideas without even having taken a good look at them. Now, it might be fine to take naturalism on board as your *position*, which you bring into conversation with other large-scale metaphysical positions in philosophy, all without claiming that naturalism has yet been made worthy of belief, but the latter claim is another matter: it is premature.

It's important to see how contrary to the spirit of science any other behavior here must be. Science had its beginnings when with fervent curiosity human beings became open to many more ways things could be than were represented in the orthodoxies of the day, such as the cosmogonies of the Greek myths. Naturalism is an orthodoxy of intellectual culture today, and it is in the spirit of science to resist being constricted by it in our intellectual endeavors. Of course, it's a huge *compliment* to science to insist that all of reality can be understood by means of scientific inquiry. But true science is humble, and will refuse the compliment.

A transition

If naturalistic belief is questionable, then so, of course, is the naturalistic shortcut to atheism. It's true that getting rid of the anti-God rhetoric we tangled with in the previous chapter makes naturalism more of a contender in this regard than it could otherwise be. But it may be that a lot of its persuasiveness—meaning its power to persuade, not its right to do so—hinged precisely on that rhetoric. Naturalism, arm in arm with science, charging to the front of the crowd, leaving all that ignoble religious thinking behind. This is the popular picture. And it delivers the sense that non-naturalistic and religious ideas, whether old or new, aren't worth investigating. But such a move, as Bertrand Russell once said in another connection, "has all the advantages of theft over honest toil." A lot more intellectual toil will be required before naturalism can become plausible enough to make a defense of atheistic belief in its name rationally appealing.

What we need, then, if we want a reliable road to atheism, is something different. It will have to come from somewhere else and take us in a new direction before depositing us at atheism's door. Anti-God atheism is simply confused. Naturalistic atheism, as we've just seen, is premature, and too restrictive given the intellectual needs of the present moment. Moreover, it causes people to think—and wrongly think—that the most relevant and maybe the most powerful arguments against the existence of God start from science or from facts about the natural world such as evolution, and leads them to ignore arguments for atheism of a different provenance. As we leave the dead-end road of anti-God atheism and the shortcut of naturalism behind and begin to consider another approach, we will see that although such natural and evolutionary considerations do have a role to play in an atheistic strategy more likely to be successful, it is not a fundamental role. More fundamental is the role of quite another sort of evolution than that customarily associated with Darwin.

4

Unexplored Territory: Moral Evolution

God and evolution. Ever since Charles Darwin revolutionized the world of science with his novel idea of how evolution works, those two have often been mentioned in the same breath. Darwin's idea—the extraordinarily fruitful idea of natural selection—has been called the best idea anyone ever had, and many have thought that it puts God out of a job. Though Darwin himself was too cautious to be a metaphysical naturalist, naturalists from his time to ours have rejoiced at how his idea plugs certain apparent holes in their case. Where's the need to appeal to a deity's intending things to be such-and-so if by means of natural selection we can naturally explain why things are as they are, paying attention to every intricate detail as we do so, showing how the vast web of plant and animal life came to assume its present shape over aeons of time? Indeed, once you've acquainted yourself with modern biology, which has put Darwin's idea to work in innumerable rich and sophisticated ways, the idea of God saying "Let it be!" can appear rather childish and simpleminded by comparison.

Now, you might alter this, as many believers in effect have done, holding that God said, "Let evolution by natural selection be!" or (in a variation) "Let evolution by natural selection with occasional tweaks by me to get things exactly right be!" Even then, many atheists would say, God looks a bit unattractive—in the first case because evolution's messiness, which takes nothing away from its marvelousness when evolution is conceived as a purely natural process, seems a tad helter-skelter when it is conceived as the product of Mind, and in the second case because if God did a really bang-up job of creating and designing, tweaking and tinkering should surely not be necessary.

But that's biological evolution. And although it's often seen as a serious threat to belief in God, precisely where such anti-God sentiments can be found wafting through typical presentations of the threat, an opening for theists to respond can be detected. For if it's really *God*, a perfect personal being, who's behind things, then there must be some pretty good reasons, maybe ones we couldn't understand, for our world to be an evolutionary world. Any alert and sophisticated theist—certainly any theist in philosophy—will have internalized the basic pro-God notion and point out what I've been defending in previous chapters: that God couldn't *be* unattractive, and so confusions have to be involved in any response to the God idea presupposing otherwise. Better for the atheist just to come right out and say that given evolution, God doesn't exist, because no perfectly good God would want an evolutionary world. Unfortunately, then the atheist is also stuck with showing that what look like shortcomings in a helter-skelter evolutionary world don't just reflect our limited understanding of a good God's reasons. Discussions of the theological import of biological evolution that reach this point often end in a stalemate—or else in exchanges unworthy of inquiry, involving sarcasm and verbal abuse.

But again I say: that's just *biological* evolution. The science of evolution does have something important to tell us that we've not yet heard clearly. It will come back into our discussion secondarily later on. But I don't think we'll make really serious progress in inquiry about God and evolution unless we start by thinking about human *moral* evolution, an evolution in our understanding of what it takes to be a really good person that happens to have serious though generally unrecognized religious consequences.

It's tempting to see a parallel with Socrates and the Presocratics here. As we noted in Chapter 2, despite all their amazing innovations and their contributions to the rise of science, the Presocratics ended up in Socrates's shade. I haven't yet told you why. At least part of the reason is that subsequent thinkers decided there was more waiting to be figured out than the metaphysical and quasi-scientific puzzles with which the Presocratics concerned themselves, and that Socrates had a handle on what this was. Plato's *Phaedo* has Socrates saying that in his youth he had been disappointed by the teaching of Presocratics like Anaxagoras because it didn't tell him much about his own most urgent concern: how to live. Because he devoted his own thinking to this question and dug up a lot of interesting ideas, Socrates became closely linked to the important subject of ethics or moral philosophy—as closely as the Presocratics are to metaphysics—and because he lived (and died) with such integrity, he has been much admired by later philosophers, right down to the present day. He is often presented to students as a model philosopher.

Now, seeing that beyond metaphysics there's ethics, as Socrates and the "Postsocratics" did, is a bit like recognizing moral evolution on the other side of biological evolution. That's the parallel I'm after. Moral evolution is one aspect of the broad phenomenon customarily distinguished from biological or genetic evolution and given the label "cultural evolution." In this chapter we're going to get better acquainted with this aspect of cultural evolution. Cultural evolution doesn't have to be progressive, but in the case of moral evolution it appears that it often has been. Let's begin by seeing why we might want to say that, and then consider whether the inclination is defensible.

Moral progress

One bright afternoon last spring I drove past the spot in Halifax, Nova Scotia, where once stood a "hanging tree." Here people would gather, perhaps with children and lunch pails, to watch and cheer while men had the life choked out of them by a rope. I thought about how, in many parts of the world, this sort of thing no longer happens. Even those who today favor the execution of murderers would shudder just as I shuddered—and as I may have made you shudder—to recall how public executions were staged and enjoyed in the good old days.

We think of such changes as marking moral progress. Appreciation and respect for the value and dignity of complex life, a sensitivity to suffering, the resolve to avoid harm-involving solutions to social problems wherever possible, the aim to develop humanitarian impulses in ourselves and in our children—all of these things are today regarded as desirable and valuable, though they have not always been clearly recognized as such; more and more they are visible in human lives. And none is as well honored in a world where public executions take place as in one from which they have been banned, as they were banned from Canada in 1869.

In his book *The Ethical Project*, the philosopher Philip Kitcher goes quite a bit further back for his first example of moral progress than 1869. Over a few centuries in the ancient Near East a transition occurred from a literal "eye for an eye" practice, or the *lex talionis*, in which, for example, the wife of a rapist might be raped by someone chosen by the father of the victim, to a practice that involved going after the perpetrator directly. How can the new understanding and behavior here not reflect moral progress, asks Kitcher, given that in the earlier practice someone is caught up in the "machinery of punishment" who had nothing to do with the action being punished?

Kitcher has other examples. He mentions a shift in ancient Greece from focusing on personal honor in warfare, which came to appear selfish and irresponsible, to the disciplined pursuit, in battle, of the good of the group. A small shift, you may think, but still a shift. The past 2,000 years have also seen a greater valuing of compassion in the West, in part due to the influence of Christianity. Dramatically progressive shifts are those that more recently have almost everywhere produced a deep resistance to slavery; a recognition of the equality of women with men and their mutual responsibilities in every field of human activity, including the home (we are still working at internalizing this one); and dispositions favoring what Kitcher calls "the withering of vice"—in particular, greater acceptance of gay sex and the desires it presupposes as nondeviant (here's another shift we're still navigating). Other examples of moral progress that might be mentioned are the changes involved in the slow transition from oppressive authoritarian regimes to freedom-respecting democracies and our growing concern not just for our own well-being and that of our families and our local groups but for the well-being of human beings and other sentient creatures everywhere.

Notice that each example of moral progress I've mentioned is marked by a kind of *subtraction*. We subtract from our picture of moral goodness—and try to subtract from our behavior—something that had previously been taken for granted, because of a new sensitivity to what's wrong with it. We subtract the favoring of (as well as any tolerance for) killing of human beings in public, "eye for an eye" punishment, honor killing and dying, demeaning cruelty, slavery, sexism, demonizing of gays, governmental authoritarianism, and partial and arbitrarily discriminating care. And with each of these you have the more subtle subtractions making it possible, such as the subtraction of callous and rude insensitivity toward other people's feelings, of unthinking prejudice and undiscriminating retributivism, of tolerated class distinctions and unquestioning obedience to physically powerful authority, of patronizing attitudes toward women and the feminine, and of an accepted relational "distance" on the part of fathers and other men.

There is a more general category of progress we can see in most of the cases of progressive subtraction I've just listed. This involves a *movement away from violence*. Go through those cases again and you'll see what I mean: violence is often the cause of such things or expressed in them. So a more basic point to be made here concerns violence: it appears to have declined. And we think it would be wonderful if we could subtract more of it.

With optimism properly kept cautious but with mountains of data, Steven Pinker, in his *The Better Angels of Our Nature*—the book that (as explained in the Preface) had something to do with my decision to write this one—supports the notion that violence and the conditions that make for violence have indeed declined among us. Over the course of history, we can see reductions of violence because of factors promoting less tribal raiding and feuding, less homicide and other violent crime, less slavery and cruel punishment and religious persecution, less great-power and interstate war, less civil war, genocide, and autocracy. And then there are all the reductions in violence to be associated with a host of recent "Rights Revolutions" focused on "civil rights, women's rights, children's rights, gay rights, and animal rights." Of course, finite and limited as we are, it's easy to be influenced by destructive things that happened yesterday or last week to wonder whether a truly significant reduction in violence has been achieved; some of Pinker's readers *have* wondered. But he convincingly defends the idea that when we try to think in something more like species time than in human time, we'll notice that, for many dimensions of violence and by many measures, what he calls our better angels—empathy, self-control, the moral sense, and reason—

have indeed been having an impact in the world of vulnerable flesh and blood.

As Pinker shows, violence was once taken for granted and treated much more casually. He tells of how in sixteenth-century Paris the slow roasting of wailing cats was considered good clean fun. But good people today just as naturally oppose violence in all the spheres of life, and do what they can to hasten the day when it will be, if not altogether eliminated, at least much further diminished still. Even when it comes to the formerly reluctant acceptance of violence as instrumentally necessary—that is, necessary as a means to valuable ends, such as criminal justice—we are seeing changes. More and more good people are concluding that, with imagination and resourcefulness, we can find alternatives to violence for most if not all ends worth pursuing.

Speaking of good people, it's now time to see how these changes we've been talking about, as suggested at various points along the way, all involve changes to our conception of what really good people are like and how they are disposed to behave—or, because of the subtractions, *not* disposed to behave. Consider those human beings whom we regard as morally exemplary. It can be useful to make a list of such moral exemplars, the individuals one would most readily be inclined to call really good people, in whom the relevant qualities stand out most clearly. (They don't have to be perfect—that would make for a short list.) On my list appear some religious and social activists such as Jesus of Nazareth—at least as seen through the lens of biblical criticism, and when he wasn't in a bad mood, cursing fig trees. Martin Luther King, Jr. belongs there too. And Abraham Lincoln makes my list, as do Florence Nightingale, Gandhi, Eleanor Roosevelt, and Elie Wiesel. I deeply admire the universalizing empathy and compassion of Jesus and Florence Nightingale, King's passion for justice and for the dignity of the oppressed, Lincoln's sympathy, Gandhi's social idealism,

Roosevelt's insistence that the rights of all people be respected, and Wiesel's determination that horrors such as the Holocaust shall be prevented from ever happening again. These are people who—at least in some respect—can leave us in a state of moral awe when we read about their lives. It seems that the world is so much better for their having lived. Differences in moral emphasis are invited by reflection on their lives. But there are also some common strands. These include deep compassion and appropriate empathy toward all other people (or even all living beings) and unstinting efforts to remove obstacles to the realization of our potential and preservation of our dignity. Thinking about such dispositions as realized in actual humans and the subtractions required to get there provides living evidence of the progress I've been concerned to elucidate—while also confirming our inclination to call it progress.

Evolution and *progress*? Or just evolution?

But right here a question may seem to arise. Why should we think any of these changes I've been drawing attention to really amounts to moral *progress*, with the strong positive evaluation that implies, instead of just change or evolution? People who write about cultural evolution are sometimes criticized for slipping all too easily from "evolution" to "progress." Contemporary work on the subject—for example, Tim Lewens's recent book *Cultural Evolution* and also the very influential and often collaborative writing on cultural evolution of Peter Richerson and Robert Boyd—is very sensitive to this issue and distances itself quite consciously and deliberately from the assumption that cultural change has to be for the good and result in ever more positive and valuable conditions over time. (By the way, it also often and wisely emphasizes how little we yet know about how cultural evolution works. Certainly no straight analogy with how biological evolution works seems to hold water.)

I think it's important that we avoid an overreaction here: even if cultural evolution isn't inherently or intrinsically progressive, or *steadily* progressive, it can still involve marked improvements over time relative to a variety of aims, as it evidently has done in the realm of technology, and it may more often and more reliably be made progressive as we learn more about how it works—books like Lewens's (and those he cites) will help us do so—and on that basis get people effectively mobilized around clear and important cultural goals. But this might still leave one wondering whether it's really been progressive in producing the *moral* instances I've offered as examples of progress. How could one try to show this?

Three points suggest themselves, and between them make for a powerful case. One involves the notion of reasons. Although thinking about goodness is importantly different from thinking about matters addressed by human science and technology, both involve *giving reasons*. From the moment we wake up we're evaluating and at least implicitly thinking of reasons for doing or being this instead of that. It's just part of acquiescing in human life (you can't stop it except by exiting that category). We can at most do it better—notice the evaluation even here! And that our reasoning about such matters has improved can't be denied. For example, as a species we've learned, and more and more individual humans now learn as they grow up, that it's arbitrary and so unreasonable—sometimes we'll say "discriminatory"—to withhold respectful treatment from other people in relevant respects no different from ourselves. Such things as universal declarations of human rights, which we all know about, are evidence of this. Thus moral progress, at bottom, should be regarded as nothing more than rational progress, and no one will deny that we have a capacity for *that*.

This first point can be filled out and strengthened. Some of the moral learning we've done over time comes from the thinking of philosophers who have developed moral theories. Though rather different from scientific theories, moral theories too are products of intellectual and rational activity. So what do we find when we consult them? You may think that because of the disagreement among philosophers, more evident than disagreement in science, a clear answer to this question will not be forthcoming. But there's an easy way around this apparent difficulty. We can look for areas of *overlap*—for views relevant to the issue of moral progress that *all* these theories, whatever their other differences, can be seen to share. And, as it happens, all of the most influential forms of theoretical reasoning about morality today lend themselves to the support of "subtractions" like those I earlier associated with moral progress.

Moral theories have to be either *consequentialist* or *nonconsequentialist*, that is, they'll either make rightness and wrongness a matter entirely of the consequences of an action, or they won't do so. We can check with the most prominent views in both camps to see whether the point I just made is true.

In the consequentialist camp, we find *social contract theory*, which tells us it's in our rational self-interest to submit to rules promoting social harmony; one can argue for at any rate many of the subtractions from this base. The same goes for *utilitarianism*, a very influential theory which permits us to reason to the correctness of many of our subtractions from its starting point, which involves a bracingly undiscriminating concern for well-being and flourishing.

In the nonconsequentialist camp, we find *Kantian ethics*, named for the great eighteenth-century German philosopher Immanuel Kant, whose most comprehensible version of the famous "Categorical Imperative" has it that we must always treat ourselves and others with respect, which Kant cashes out in terms of treating people always as ends and never as means only. Many of the subtractions, clearly, can be justified by thinking about what it takes to be respectful to ourselves and others in this way. Finally, in the same camp we have *virtue ethics* (sometimes today appearing in a self-consciously feminist form) which tells us that morality is more about who we are—the virtues we possess or vices we betray—than what we do, and a short look at even a long list of the dispositions today regarded as virtues will confirm that by this approach too the subtractions come out as rationally justified. Moreover, it is evident that the qualities I earlier mentioned in connection with moral exemplars—such things as empathy and sympathy, compassion and justice—are going to be conspicuously present on any such list.

Now, that one of these consequentialist or nonconsequentialist moral theories (or some combination) has it at least approximately right is what we should assume, for otherwise philosophical inquiry—itself urged on us by reason—could hardly proceed. Otherwise we'd have to say that none of our most important ideas has any merit, and that would rather strongly suggest that further inquiry is hopeless. Even more noteworthy, perhaps, as a reason for making the assumption in question is the fact that consequentialism and nonconsequentialism are logically the only options! Every moral theory has got to fall into one category or the other. Moreover, every consequentialist theory must either be grounded in self-interest or in the interests of all, and there could hardly be a nonconsequentialist theory that, having turned away from exclusive attention to the consequences of our actions, did not look to other features of human behavior, such as our motives and desires, as virtue theory does. Because the theories we have cover these bases, we should therefore suppose that one of them or some combination is at least approximately right. But they all support the idea of moral progress. Thus, despite the disagreement among our theories, we may make use of that support, concluding that moral reason broadly endorses the idea that moral progress has occurred.

A second point that can be used to defend moral progress, one that might succeed even if the first one failed, applies something you learn early on in any course on moral theory: that not just general moral ideas (commonly called principles) are needed to rationally generate a moral judgment but also some sense of the nonmoral *facts* of the case. For example, to conclude, using the moral principle that stealing is wrong, that what Joe did in taking that book from your bedside table was wrong, you need the completely nonmoral and purely factual premise that what Joe did in taking that book amounts to stealing. This opens up an interesting possibility. Maybe a great many of the changes we are calling "moral evolution" can count as progress even if there's little or no change (and so little or no progress) at the level of moral principles, which are usually the focus of moral theory. Maybe much of it happens at the level of nonmoral fact instead, where everyone will agree our understanding can improve.

To a surprising extent, this thought is borne out by investigation. We often arrive at new moral beliefs just by seeing the nonmoral facts differently. For example, we learn new facts about the subtle and long-lasting diminishments of happiness that come from casual violence, or about the abilities of women, or about the needs of children, or about the sincere desire of many gay men and women for loving monogamous relationships, or about the promise of nonviolent solutions to conflict, or about the intelligence and sensitivity of slaves, once regarded as brutes—or about the sensitive emotional lives of the nonhuman animals we still think of as "brutes." These are all nonmoral matters. Such ordinary improvements in our factual understanding drive us to bring new situations under old moral principles (for example, we may bring cats under a principle of care that formerly excluded them). And so we have new moral results and also moral progress—for, after all, we've subtracted clear errors from our moral thinking.

My third point is the simplest, and might have been dialectically effective all on its own. I adapt it from Steven Pinker's more general follow-up to *Better Angels*, called *Enlightenment Now*. Pinker suggests that the issue we've raised is a kind of pseudo-issue, since, after all, every one of us swims in this moral stream of cultural evolution. The set of people who really doubt that we've made moral progress, who might honestly stand behind the concern we've raised, has zero members. To advert to some earlier examples: pretty well everyone agrees that modern forms of punishment are better than killing human beings in public or "an eye for an eye," that freedom is better than slavery, and that kindness is better than cruelty. We agree because we see that our aims for ourselves are, in each case, better served by the one thing than by the other, and because we've learned that people everywhere *share* our own most general aims and have come to believe that they deserve just as much as we do to see them realized. But if we all agree about such things, then no special defense of moral progress is needed.

Now, a note of caution is called for here with regard to how much I should be taken to be claiming when I speak of progress in this book. I've said that the progress I'm interested in is progress in our understanding of what it takes to be *a really good person*. This is because of the obvious connection to the idea of moral perfection in the theist's conception of God. That we've made such progress is compatible with regression in other areas, and so my story of progress is not as wide a progressive story as Pinker's. It's even compatible with regression in certain moral areas. We don't have to say that everything is peachy-keen in Western democratic societies (not that Pinker does). We can critique, say, individualism and consumerism, among any number of other features of contemporary culture. Being optimistic about progress in one area doesn't require you to be similarly optimistic in all areas. It could be that some will think we *need* a story about how we are in general making moral progress and about the evolutionary mechanisms enabling this, if we are to earn confidence in such specific claims about progress as I am making—claims about progress in our understanding of what it takes to be a really good person. But this I would deny. Such a claim can stand on its own two feet, feet which I have been shaping and solidifying in this chapter.

Is the future a problem here?

But now a new objection may beg to be heard: "Hold on! Moral evolution might very well *continue*—notice how nicely this idea fits into all that talk about human immaturity in the last chapter. And perhaps, as moral evolution continues, it will lead human beings to change their minds on some of the 'results' of moral evolution you're counting on. We've recently seen, for example, how views that many culturally sensitive people have held to most strongly as a result of changes you've referenced, for example, on our obligation to provide 'safe spaces' in colleges or put 'trigger warnings' on syllabi that even so much as mention violence, have quickly shifted under the influence of new ideas—for example, about the 'infantilization' of students treated in this way. So things move back and forth a lot, and who knows whether morality is properly conceived in terms of what prevails at this time rather than that? Maybe we've only reached an early level of moral development, and not one we can yet count on to reflect how things really are in the moral domain."

In response, I would certainly agree that it's possible people will change their minds about the moral views I've emphasized, though it seems unlikely. New sensitivities, once developed, are harder to lose than to add to. That careful moral thinking will go back to the approval of what I assume we've grown beyond—say, roasting cats for fun or strangling people in public—is even less likely than smart techies going back from today's computing devices to the Commodore 64. In any case, what needs to be made realistic here is the notion that any such moral changes, should they occur, would *rightly come to be seen as positive and progressive over the long term rather than regressive.* And the reasoning of the previous section suggests otherwise. Notice that it's not just my reasoning and my feelings, or those of a few people here and there, that strongly favor a subtraction of violence and of the other nasty things we've been talking about. As the Pinker view suggests, for the moral views in question we have quite a wide consensus, and it's likely that we'll be building on this in future moral evolution, much as we build on consensus results in science. And whether we actually do or not, we should.

It's worth noting that the <u>infantilization</u> debate doesn't help the objection. For what people who lodge protests in the name of infantilization have been saying is that sensitivity to violence can be taken too far or misapplied. They wouldn't encourage going all the way back from this to the much earlier dispositions and practices I'm assuming we've grown beyond. That would be another and far worse extreme! Indeed, the concern for avoidance of infantilization is itself a symptom of the moral progress I have pointed to, with its sharp attention to the conditions in which our potential can be realized.

In case it's needed, let me add that nothing in the arguments of this book could without caricature be construed as advocating an infantilization of the human species. The atheistic arguments to come in later chapters work perfectly well even if we are quite unhappy with the idea of a culture grown soft. Here we should beware of what amounts to a crass either-or. It's not as though either we sanction all the nasty stuff in our world or people are coddled and turned into sissies. As we'll see later, plenty of courage would be called for in many imaginable scenarios in which violence and other such things are quite absent.

Perhaps it will be argued that whatever may have happened with respect to such things as our views about violence at the level of personal or collective belief, we should avoid turning these beliefs into *judgments* that we employ in inquiry and publicly champion as I'm doing here. We should instead *suspend* judgment about how things are in the relevant respects because of the developmental immaturity mentioned by the objection, which I myself have emphasized earlier in the book.

But that would require suspending judgment as to whether we have in fact arrived at moral results from which there's no going back (as opposed to forward). And three things prevent me from finding this move persuasive in the moral realm. First, our basic stance on matters of value is deeper and more fundamental to our whole way of being in the world than our stance on, say, how the universe originated, or on whether natural selection is the primary mechanism of evolution. Suspending judgment here could render us immobile. Second, there is the consensus already mentioned about the general changes I'm emphasizing. It's in part because we're still seeking this in many areas of inquiry that our maturity there can be questioned. Though immature, if we're going to engage in inquiry at all and noticeably advance in it, we'll need to have some criterion for determining when an advance we can count on has been made. And it's hard to think of anything better than a wide and representative consensus—a meeting of minds. Third, as is often said, though we have advanced a great deal in other areas—for example, technologically—morally we have conspicuously lagged behind, and *early* advances can be easier to identify as real. Thus it's not clear that evidence of our developmental immaturity would help the objection. Such evidence might harm it instead.

Here computer technology affords another analogy. That we were moving forward was pretty obvious when we left behind computers that filled a 20-by-40-foot room and weighed 30 tons. Today, real advances in computer technology are more subtle and difficult to detect. Similarly (and ironically), it is precisely the depth of our moral immaturity that gives us a reason to think that when, for example, we wonder at human violence and strongly desire its diminishment and also its final containment or elimination, we are part of a real move out of the cave.

* * *

A white cross still hangs on the dirty back wall of the old Gloucester Laundry in Dublin. The last of Ireland's infamous Magdalene laundries, it closed in 1996 and will soon be demolished. But the indignities suffered by the women and girls confined there, some for life, won't be as easy to erase. Long hours of grueling work in cold, damp conditions with poor nutrition and hygiene and little or no medical attention—this was the norm for these women and girls. *Penance* is what the Roman Catholic nuns who ran the place called it, while sometimes adding their own punishment to what inmates were already experiencing. But penance for what? It was penance for turning to prostitution or for getting pregnant—sometimes, as Joni Mitchell sang in her song about the Laundries, by your own father— or for being an orphan or for being unwanted or abused by your family. Mortality rates at the Laundries were high; scores of women and girls have been found buried together in mass graves. In recent decades people and governments have finally become willing to do something about such horrors, and instead of silence or shunning, a small band of survivors who came to Dublin recently for a reunion found themselves greeted by cheering from a crowd on the street.

Reading about all this today in the news, I wondered what could be more obvious to me than that what happened in the Magdalene laundries was often very bad indeed, and that their closure and the associated changes in public opinion and behavior amount to real improvements. Sure, a great many social problems remain, and our own ways of dealing with them are often imperfect and call for their own fixes. Hellish circumstances of the day were detailed elsewhere in the newspaper. But here was a thinning in the fog of gloom, maybe even a small patch of light. Moral progress.

5

Updating God

The Christian New Testament tells us that the apostle Paul, while on a preaching tour that had him in Athens, noticed an altar with the inscription "TO AN UNKNOWN GOD." Good evangelist that he was, Paul seized the opportunity: "This God you ignorantly worship, I declare unto you." Paul certainly thought he knew what he was talking about and that only his audience was uninformed. But because of a connection between progressive moral evolution of the sort described in the last chapter and human thinking about God, it turns out that he was mistaken. Ironically, the God Paul worshiped was unknown to *Paul*.

How could this be? Didn't Paul know that his idea of God was that of a perfect personal being, a being with measureless power, knowledge, and goodness? Yes, presumably he did. He was writing about it all the time, in letters that are now themselves in the New Testament. So what's the problem? Well, as we've just seen, human moral evolution has generated, since Paul's time, a conception of admirable personhood rather different from Paul's. It has changed our standards of goodness in ways we should all approve. And if that's so, then our idea of God's goodness has to change too. *It has to be updated.* Paul's God, for example, is very concerned to display his glory; plans that some people will share in it and that others will be thrown away, like a lump of clay from the potter's wheel; and has enemies who will feel the violence of "His" wrath. But now suppose we assume that what we've learned about moral goodness can be applied to God. Then we'd have to say that God's moral nature is rather different. Then much of it was unknown to Paul. He was talking about God without really knowing who he was talking about.

Paul has had lots of company. For most of its history, the debate about God has featured debaters who literally didn't know what they were talking about. On one side we've had God-believers talking about God without being able—sometimes without being willing—to work into their understanding of a perfect personal being what the species has slowly been picking up about moral matters. On the other side, we've had God-doubters and God-deniers. As we saw in Chapter 2, especially at the level of popular discussion such nonbelievers haven't always thought about the idea of God very carefully, and neither in popular nor in philosophical discussion have they taken account of the motives and behavior our recent moral development suggests would be found in God, were there to be one. Though the concept of evolution has emerged among them, nonbelievers have been far more concerned about biological than about moral evolution. And even when they themselves have displayed the effects of the latter, it has generally been while assuming that a creditable conception of a perfectly good God wouldn't need to. So nonbelievers too have been talking about an unknown God.

Believers like Paul and nonbelievers like those to whom he preached could, of course, hardly have thought much about moral evolution of any kind. Of the most recent developments they obviously could have nary a clue. But believers and nonbelievers of our own time will have to find another excuse.

A great gulf fixed?

Perhaps someone will now *offer* some excuses—objections to the idea of a connection between us and God of the sort that my argument about moral evolution will allege. (And note that when speaking of moral evolution hereafter, I will mean progressive moral evolution of the sorts we were talking about in the previous chapter.) Might it be that instead of a connection a great gulf is fixed between our moral nature and that belonging to any God there may be? Before developing the argument any further, let's have a look at some ways of trying to show this and why they fail.

First up is the idea that an accurate understanding of a divine being's goodness would be simply out of reach for all of us—a being answering to the description of God, a perfect being with all power, all knowledge, and all goodness, would in many respects truly be an unknown God. Divinity is too far removed from humanity for us to identify more than its outlines, as we've just done. In saying this we don't have to presuppose that God actually exists. We're talking about an idea generated by humans. But it's the ultimate idea. And finite humans have to live with the fact that in generating such an exalted idea, they have also put out of reach what the content of the idea would amount to were it realized. Of course, this doesn't help Paul, but it does introduce a new kind of "uninformed" condition and spread it around in such a way that my arguments won't do any better, in terms of conveying the nature of God, than Paul's preaching.

The answer to this objection is that the idea of God is not the ultimate or most basic religious idea but rather a *version* of it, through which we humans have added to more fundamental notions the comprehensible content associated with personhood. Of course, we in the West often treat the idea of theism as if it were the fundamental religious idea, but that, as we saw two chapters back, has to do with a kind of spiritual ethnocentrism reflecting immaturity on our part; the idea of a divine reality could be—and has been—developed in many other ways.

So what is that more general and fundamental religious idea, to which theism stands much as the specific versions of it found in the theistic religions of the world—Christian theism, Islamic theism, and so on—stand to theism itself? There are actually several possibilities (we'll discuss them more fully in Chapter 10). Many would here speak with an understandable vagueness of a "transcendent reality" or of an "ultimate reality" or of an "ultimate divine reality." I myself have proposed that, at any rate going forward, and for purposes of religious investigation, we might link religion to a less vague proposition I call *ultimism*. Whatever its status, ultimism is indeed a religious proposition, and more fundamental than theism. It says that a divine reality would have three broad and interrelated characteristics, each representing a type of ultimacy: its existence would be the ultimate fact about the nature of reality; it would embody the ultimate in inherent value; and it would at least potentially be the source of an ultimate good for the world.

Returning to theism, we can see that it assumes ultimism but through its notion of personhood and agency provides more information than ultimism alone does; we might call this elaboration of ultimism *theistic* ultimism or *personal* ultimism. According to theism, God is a personal creator who intentionally produces or permits everything else that exists (ultimate fact); who has all power, all knowledge, and all goodness (ultimate inherent value); and whose love—a part of personal moral goodness as defined in Chapter 1— makes for our deepest well-being (source of an ultimate good).

Theism therefore represents one way of filling out the more general idea of ultimism, drawing on ideas we understand and can examine for their truth-value. There might still be a good reason to say that the content of ultimism itself is out of our reach, provided we exclude theism, for then we'd have to say that some other elaboration must apply from the many elaborations, both extant and undeveloped, that could be offered for so general a notion; and we might very well have no idea *which* applies, at least at an early and immature stage of religious investigation. But this still leaves theism with a quite different status, and the objection without a leg to stand on.

A second objection argues that God's goodness can't be judged by the standards of our morality. What someone who says this might mean is that God can do whatever God likes because, after all, God is God! Who are we to say that God would or should do otherwise? There's an error here that isn't hard to diagnose: people are sometimes—and especially in the religious case—tempted to say that "might is right" when it isn't. The possession of all power wouldn't give a God a moral *carte blanche*. When we say that God is perfectly good as well as all-powerful we do indeed add something, something that should make a God appear to us most deeply wonderful as well as awesome in a strictly power-oriented way. And "wonderful" is our concept; we humans get to give it the content we want it to have. Here *we* have the power!

But isn't it somehow still impious for humans to judge a being who, if it existed, would be their creator? The problem here is with the expression "judge a being": it suggests that we're adopting an attitude of authority over God, who would, of course, if existent, have authority over us. Arguments like mine don't require anything of the sort. All they require is that we make judgments about—that is, say what we think is true about—what God's goodness would include or exclude. Notice how this sort of judging is rather different from the sort of quasi-legal "sitting in judgment on" that the objector has in mind; it's more closely related to believing. And notice that it is directed not to God—as though we could in such an investigation just assume that there is one!—but rather to the *idea* of God.

Perhaps, however, we should take our second objection to be pointing to a more subtle notion, which even some theologians have endorsed: that the expression "good" when applied to God has a different meaning from "good" when applied in ordinary human contexts. This pretty quickly leads to the suspicion that we can't really know what we're *saying* when we call God good, which brings us back within the ambit of the first objection and also my replies to it—in particular, the worry about confusing theism with ultimism. But some additional replies might be made here.

At least in philosophy—where, as noted in Chapter 1, our inclination must be to carve out a precise idea so we can investigate its possible relevance as an answer to fundamental questions—we need to know what we're talking about. We *decide* what we're going to be talking about, and in the case of theism we decide that we're going to explore the idea that the most fundamental reality is a person, extrapolating from our ordinary concept of personhood, which includes agency, consciousness, and moral status. And if we say that an ultimate person would be perfectly good, we mean that in much the same sense employed in other contexts. Of course, we can imagine a being whose "goodness" corresponded to some unknown quantity, maybe a condition we'll know about a million years from now. But that's no help to investigation now. If a God would be "good" but only in that other unknown sense, then all bets are off and investigation must cease—which completely defeats the purpose we had when introducing the idea in the first place.

Notice that even if "good" has the same meaning in the human and divine cases, a God's goodness might still be different from ours in lots of ways; we wouldn't just be turning God into an enlarged hominin. For God's goodness would be maximally great (ours isn't);

God, being omnipotent, would necessarily prevent unjustified evil (the most even a perfectly good human could do would be to resist it) and would not be acting through a physical body restricted to a portion of space; being omniscient, moreover, God would have a perfectly accurate understanding of all the facts involving good and evil (ours is fallible and liable to err). Various such differences must indeed be acknowledged, but that still leaves "good" meaning the same thing in the two cases, and leaves our standards of goodness applicable to talk about God's. By the same token, if our standards change, our understanding of God's goodness may rightly change too.

But this just leads into a third objection. Our standards of goodness change because we are *humble hominins*, it may be said, facing various challenges set by evolution in a terrestrial environment. It is indeed as a *response* to distinctively human problems that our morality and its alterations arise. How can we suppose that standards of behavior intended to solve specifically human problems could properly be applied to a being who, if it existed, would quite obviously face no such problems?

I agree that there is rather a large difference between us and any God here, but it is like the differences just mentioned, which don't prevent our standards from being relevant. We limited humans, working on human problems, are often prevented by a kind of intellectual shrubbery, evolutionarily produced, from *seeing* various truths or seeing them clearly until the shrubbery is trimmed. As suggested in the last chapter, these might be truths about general moral principles (this is often what is meant by talk of "standards" in this connection) or they might be truths about nonmoral facts. They might also be truths about the moral judgments that follow from the combination of those two. So, for example, some slave trader in 1797 might not have seen that *every* person should be treated with respect and dignity (moral principle) or that the individuals taken as slaves are persons (nonmoral fact) or that it follows from the previous two points, taken together, that those individuals should be treated with respect and dignity (moral judgment). Of course, we humans also face the liability that when we clearly see such truths we often still can't bring ourselves to act on them. Indeed, one of the characteristically human problems to which moralists have to respond is our propensity to do things that are morally wrong!

These points suggest a response to the third objection. God, when judging and acting, would always know what's relevantly true; this wouldn't be obscured or, in fits and starts, progressively revealed. And God certainly wouldn't face the situations that the corresponding limitations so regularly have created for us, nor would God ever fail to do the good. But this wouldn't prevent God from knowing that in a situation of type X (maybe a human situation) this or that ought to be done, or from knowing that the principles and nonmoral facts we have laboriously had to discover are real or true. More to the point, if a principle like the one I used as an example is properly accepted by us, then it *can* be applied to any God there may be: God too would realize that every person—which includes but certainly is not restricted to every human there may be—ought to be treated with dignity and respect. Of course, if there were a God, this would always have been known to God even though in the actual world we have come to see it, or see it clearly, only at some point in the course of human history.

An analogy may help. We assume that deep truths of mathematics and physics are progressively being discerned by mathematicians and physicists. Distinctively human intellectual needs call them forth, and strange human circumstances fill the books that tell us about such discoveries. Now, God never would make discoveries like that or apply them as scientists do or have to negotiate the odd twists and turns of human intellectual life. Yet, if there is a God, all such truths are constantly available to the divine mind, since a God would be omniscient. And if relevant, say, to some task of universe-building, necessary truths of mathematics must apply even to a God's activities. In the same way, despite the messy circumstances of human moral existence and the limitations that attend every human moral doing, when moral truths are discovered they are truths that a God would always have known. The contingent facts of human life may make it seem otherwise. But here again we have the intellectual shrubbery.

Evolution of the God idea

Objections to the connection I am forging between changes in human moral standards and changes to our conception of God's goodness therefore do not withstand scrutiny. Indeed, the last objection, all things considered, might be seen as giving this book's argument a decided boost. Our status as <u>immature hominins</u> means that when we leave some morally relevant notion behind, it is tainted with that immaturity, and surely we can be confident that *such* things ought to be excluded from our conception of a perfectly good person. It makes no sense to think of the character of a perfectly good being as including what we ourselves have outgrown. If we focus on these things—on the "subtractions" as I have called them, and on any qualities entailed by their subtraction—extrapolations to God must certainly be safe.

So let's get back to the God connection. We might express what's going on here by saying that moral evolution should lead to a kind of *religious* evolution. But there are at least two kinds of religious evolution involving God, and we should make sure we've distinguished them. The first kind is illustrated by the work of Karen Armstrong. A prolific and well-known religious writer and ex-nun,

Armstrong explores how religious ideas have changed in books with titles like *The History of God* and *The Great Transformation*. Though many people around the world still believe in a personal God, she will tell you that this is just one of many ways in which the notion of a divine reality has been understood. There are many more items on the religious menu. Armstrong can appear quite enthusiastic about them and quite down on the idea of a personal God. She is exploring forms of religious evolution *beyond* God.

Such work on evolution beyond God is becoming more common. But it should be distinguished from the kind of evolution we're starting to get acquainted with here, which is far less familiar—and indeed generally overlooked. The first kind of religious change or evolution in the West, Armstrong's kind, would take us beyond the personal God idea into other regions of the transcendent. But the unrecognized second kind involves a kind of expansion, sophistication, refinement of the personal God idea itself. The first sort of evolution, as I've said, we can call evolution beyond God. The second we might call the evolution *of* God—or, more accurately, of the God idea.

To understand how this second sort of evolution is possible, we need to notice the difference between positive evaluations such as "morally all good," which appear in our definition of "God," and the *criteria or standards* we apply when determining what it takes to live up to such descriptions. When discussing the nature and existence of God we can discuss how things would be with a personal God were such a being to exist and to be perfectly good. And here's the thing. Although if our focus is a personal God, the emphasis on perfect goodness won't change or evolve, the standards by which we determine what kind of character and behavior would *count* as perfectly good may change. These can evolve.

As we've seen, they are evolving today, in ways that are directly applicable to the God debate, allowing for an evolution of our idea of

God that no one appears to be ready for. This may be because of the prevalence of a certain assumption: the assumption that the personal God idea is an old idea, and that how the idea of God's goodness is to be interpreted and understood is accordingly to be determined by how in days of old people spoke and wrote about God. But this assumption is mistaken. The definition of God, in addressing the moral attributes of the deity, says no more than that God would be perfectly good. And as our species matures, morally speaking, we naturally have to update our understanding of what such goodness would include and exclude.

So how must the idea of God evolve? Well, consider again the "subtractions" of the last chapter. What dispositions and behaviors are we leaving behind, as artifacts of our species' moral immaturity? Here is a partial list: demeaning and barbaric killing, cruelty, slavery, sexism, demonizing of gays, authoritarianism, partial and arbitrarily discriminating care, rude insensitivity toward other people's feelings, prejudice and undiscriminating retributivism, patronizing attitudes toward women and the feminine, insensitivity to the importance of loving relationships, and an easy acceptance of a relational "distance" on the part of men. More generally, we saw how *violence* has to be left behind. And with respect to some paradigms of goodness a few other subtractions can be noted. You don't get to the universal empathy and compassion of a Jesus or a Florence Nightingale without shedding callous indifference and ceasing to distance yourself from others' feelings, or to a Martin Luther King's passion for justice without leaving *in*justice behind, or to a Lincoln's sympathy without losing uncaring, unsympathetic tendencies, or to a Gandhi's idealism without rejecting moral and social timidity, or to an Eleanor Roosevelt's concern for universal human rights without ceasing to uphold favoritism and partiality or tolerate disrespectful behavior, or to a Wiesel's resistance of Holocaust horrors without getting past the relative equanimity or resigned acquiescence many in the past have shown when others have suffered greatly and people's lives have been torn apart.

What would happen if we methodically subtracted all such things from the character profile of God, leaving aside those emphases of the past that reflect a relatively crude and unrefined moral mentality? Although we've tended not to do so, instead resting content with static theological pictures from the past, we can and should use such changes to improve our understanding of what a good God would oppose. Thus no longer, for example, do we need to deny the literal truth of the "Noah and the Ark" story by pointing out geographical or biological or engineering implausibilities. Just the undiscriminating retributivism which swept children and other innocents away in the flood and the callous insensitivity to suffering, not to mention the sanctioning of Noah's unquestioning submission to powerful authority, is quite sufficient. These things show for people whose morality has appropriately evolved that a perfect being whose moral goodness is unsurpassable could not possibly devise or execute such plans.

Let's now think a bit more generally. It was once quite casually assumed that a personal being could be completely, perfectly, *unsurpassably* good (and presumably also—because omniscient— unsurpassably imaginative and resourceful) while designing a home for life that is red in tooth and claw and human hand. Those who said that there was no other way for God to achieve multiple good ends God might have in view, such as significant moral freedom, were readily heard and approved. But standards of goodness have changed—appropriately so! And this has consequences for how we today can think of God's goodness. One cannot rationally think it is of the essence of personal moral goodness to oppose violence without admitting that God would oppose it too, presumably far more successfully. And this no matter how much more tolerant of violence were earlier pictures of how a morally perfect God might behave. If we grow, morally speaking, the idea of God has to grow too.

Notice how Darwin's theory of evolution by natural selection, which tells us that nature was <u>incredibly violent</u> for long aeons before *huh?* *Homo sapiens* came on the scene, suddenly snaps into relevance at this point. A fuller discussion will have to wait until Chapters 7 and 8. The point I want to make here is just this: you can now start to see why I have suggested that evolution through natural selection might become truly powerful in the case for atheism only if we first internalize moral evolution.

Leaving behind the Solitary Male, Distant Father, and Capricious King

Rather imperfect ideas about the character of a perfect being have lain largely undisturbed in our culture for centuries, while the materials for a much-improved conception have quietly been put in place by moral evolution. Let's now have a closer look at three of these imperfect ideas: the ideas of God as Solitary Male, Distant Father, and Capricious King. As we'll see, an updated conception of God must certainly leave these ideas behind.

God as Solitary Male is supported by the use of masculine pronouns such as "He" in church and synagogue and mosque and in religious scriptures, and the thought, present in centuries of theology, of a lone being calculating the proper dimensions and contents of a universe. The Distant Father is widely evident too, for example, in the repeated prayers of supplication offered by believers around the world and the many psalms begging God to draw near. The Capricious King is little more than ancient and authoritarian monarchies writ large, and is shored up by the sense of God as continually issuing commands (in scriptures sometimes also taking them back) and violently punishing those who fail to conform.

The overall effect is to make of God a rather dark and severe, even demanding and harsh being, quite in sync with the nature of the physical world in which theistic religion has developed but quite at odds with the picture of what really good people are like—and in particular what sorts of things they oppose—that we have seen moral evolution delivers. Yes, in some regions of religion, such as those touched by the example of Jesus, which as we noted have made their own contributions to moral evolution, there is a contrasting emphasis on gentleness and compassion. But this hasn't done away with the dark and severe God; instead, we once again have unreconciled streams of thought flowing side by side. Jesus himself, in the hands of the more dark and severe gospel writers, comes away looking less than sanguine about God's compassion for the world, as distinct from his own. We have the irony of towering religious figures and founders more sensitive to the ills of the world than could be the being to whom they pray, whom they regard as being perfect and as having created the world.

You may have noticed that each of the three big ideas I've mentioned includes masculinity. The first does so explicitly, the others implicitly, given that you can't be a father or a king without being male. So just by appreciating what it means to aim to eradicate sexism from a culture, you can already see that all three of these ideas are unworthy indications of God's nature and misleading indications of how God would be motivated and how God would behave. (Perhaps they could be retained as limited images of God to be balanced by other images, but they cannot form part of a correct conception of God—our idea of what God would *be*.) A personal God could not remain as distant from other personal beings as fathers in times past have gotten away with being. Nor could God gaze on other persons with the haughty condescension and violent proclivities of a king, using them to further divine purposes.

We can draw on other features of moral evolution to make such things perfectly clear. God would, if perfectly good, be even more opposed to disrespect for living beings than a Florence Nightingale or an Eleanor Roosevelt. And that's contrary to much of what is suggested by the three ideas under discussion here. God would be more opposed to killing and dying—whether for heroic honor or other reasons—and more generally to violence than any of us has yet succeeded in being, whereas the Solitary Male goes off to war seeking glory, and the Distant Father acquiesces in emotional estrangement, and the Capricious King makes demands on us that require us to tolerate our own death, and the death of all that matters to us, in his service.

No, with all that we have learned as our species slowly grows up, such ideas, when examined closely, turn out to be misleading and deceptive. If God would be a perfect personal being, then God would have to be a lot more admirable than that! This is what moral evolution allows us to say. And this is what atheists will say if they want the most convincing case for their stance in the God debate.

To make sure that these points reach their mark, let me diagnose and excise a misinterpretation that may be growing in some readers' minds—a misinterpretation of the general direction of reasoning in this chapter. It's pretty clear that I'm going to be suggesting that the condition of things in our world and in human life are at odds with what might be expected from God, if a God's goodness would have to live up to our enhanced standards. But why suppose that a God would be so preoccupied with *us*? Why should God's purpose for the cosmos be human-centered? Mightn't the main action be somewhere else rather than all bound up with what happens to and through beings on one planet in one galaxy in one small corner of the universe? As a friend said to me, "Maybe a God would just not be all that into us."

If we put the emphasis on the right word, I think I can agree with this sentiment: maybe a God would not be *that* into us! I agree that God's purpose might not be human-centered. And nothing I've said, correctly interpreted, points in a different direction. Indeed, a God might not create human beings or finite persons of any kind. My view requires only that God's behavior toward us, if indeed God creates beings like us, would be perfect. When thinking about how things are here on our small planet and using conditions here on the ground to test the idea that there is a God, we are naturally ourselves preoccupied with human things. But it doesn't follow at all that a *God* would have to be preoccupied with us to pass the test, even in a world in which God does create humans. At the end of the day, to preserve a proper balance, we should happily concede that what's going on with us might represent the tiniest fraction of what a God would be concerned with in a world including both God and human beings. But to allow and even emphasize that the universe would receive much more in the way of manifestations of God's goodness, we don't have to say that we would receive less. The moral goodness of an ultimate divine being would radiate in every direction limitlessly.

Darwin's neglected example

Charles Darwin is viewed in sharply different ways by people who are affected by his life and work. Many believers hate or pity him, thinking of him as inciting religious apostasy or as being sadly misled in his evolutionary thinking. Others—both believers and nonbelievers—love him, having learned what careful and fair-minded study bears out: that he was an uncommonly gentle and humble as well as truth-loving member of the species, intellectually driven but cautious and judicious when staking out a position, and generally kind to his detractors. Some atheists, in addition, see the development of his theory of evolution by natural selection as having the implication that they no less than theists are able to *explain* what happens in the world—or, even more strongly, as implying that theistic ideas must now all be consigned to the dustbin of intellectual history as a (biologically) evolutionary atheism comes into its own.

It's in part because of talk like this that a sense of deep opposition and of a strongly value-laden clash between Darwin and God can be detected in some quarters, as we noted at the beginning of the previous chapter—and not only in theistic quarters. But it's misleading talk. When, shortly before Darwin's death, two self-declared atheists of his own time, Ludwig Büchner and Edward B. Aveling, stopped by for lunch and a chat in his study, Darwin wondered why they had to be so "aggressive" in their science-based promotion of an atheistic stance. As many of his letters show, he himself was unsure whether the world of nature exhausts reality. Displaying his openness to the idea of some sort of transcendent cause, Darwin claimed his friend Huxley's newly minted label "agnostic" for himself, declaring the whole matter rather too profound for human minds to penetrate successfully.

But if Darwin was chary of having his evolutionary theorizing appropriated for atheistic ends, he nonetheless exemplifies another way in which an evolutionary approach, a rather different and *moral* evolutionary approach, can lead to atheism—one that should properly be appreciated before trying to bring biology into the picture. This is the evolution that has lately been picking up steam and is working to make all of us kinder and gentler people. Darwin's neglected example for atheists—and indeed for all of us as we consider the various ways in which atheism can be developed and defended—includes precisely this kindness and gentleness.

As his biographers never fail to observe, Darwin was extremely sensitive to the pain suffered by other creatures, including nonhuman ones. Though he had imbibed some of the mistaken racial views of his time, he was a fervent abolitionist, thinking slavery to be what it was: a dreadful abomination. One of his final acts was to provide for a weakened beetle specimen sent to him "an easy and quicker death" by putting it in a bottle with chopped laurel leaves, which he knew would release prussic acid, containing hydrogen cyanide.

The pain of his own children grieved him the most, and according to some Darwin experts it was when his own dearly beloved Annie, ten years old, died a painful death that he came to disbelieve in a good and loving personal God. If we restrict what the atheist judges false to the existence of such a being, as we've seen philosophical atheists may do, then we can say that Darwin was now an atheist. (It's because he himself seems to have been working with a broader conception that he called himself an agnostic.) It was the problem of evil that made him an atheist in my sense. And his own theory added to the evidence. When writing his autobiography he considered the pain in nature, which he knew would have to be all the greater given natural selection, and shuddered. Who, he asked, would set things up so that over aeons of time innumerable creatures live on the drawn-out agonies of other creatures? It "revolts our understanding," he wrote, to suppose that a caring and benevolent God would be the author of a world so violent and cruel.

Reading this over-swiftly, without much thought or in the grip of prejudice, one might suppose that Darwin was angry at God, or was inclined to offer up a negative evaluation of God—something like the evaluations sometimes offered up by Dawkins, the aggressive atheist of today. But, in fact, it was because Darwin thought *too much* of God—because he thought of God *too highly*—that he was unwilling to credit the thought that God could have created this world. Looking carefully at what he says, this becomes clear. And so I like to think that Darwin would have favored, over the others, the way of defending atheism we have started to expose, of which I'll be providing specimens in the next three chapters. This new way of thinking makes the connection between God and moral evolution explicit in a variety of ways, and it shows that atheism does indeed get rather a large boost from evolution: from the kind of evolution that gentle Darwin, meek and mild, exhibited but did not discover.

6

A Relationally Responsive God

The God once believed in was a majestic Male, capable of being angered and residing in distant splendor, whose tendency to remain afar off was seen as in harmony with the prerogatives of "His" Kingly nature. Such a God might think we should feel well loved simply by reflecting on the fact that we are allowed to exist at all. But what about the new idea of God? What does an updated and morally more adequate conception of God tell us about how a God would be related to us?

Our first bit of travel in the atheistic part of the territory labeled "moral evolution" is by means of an argument that answers this question. I call it the hiddenness argument. It's the argument through which, without knowing it, I think I was channeling some of the effects of moral evolution back in the early days of my own philosophizing. It's likely that the evolution reflected here had little to do with any of Darwin's thinking about God, which we were just talking about at the end of the previous chapter. In any case, it has intensified since his time and will loom larger for anyone now. But the central idea of the hiddenness argument, that not just benevolence or a concern for the good of the one loved, which may operate anonymously and from a distance, but openness to conscious relationship belongs to perfect love and thus to perfect moral goodness, can also be seen as illustrated by Darwin, who had numerous warm relationships, and loved his family dearly. Sure, he was inhibited in some cases and distractible in others, but even an occasional note or visit shows a measure of openness to relationship and relational responsiveness.

The notion that openness to relationship belongs to love is, of course, exemplified not just by Darwin but also by most of us, and generally has been—for when have humans not loved? What required cultural evolution, in relation to love, is not the appearance of love itself with its fundamental dispositions but (interrelatedly) a recognition, across a range of contexts, of the *deep value* of relational love, in a sense that involves giving of oneself and not just of one's things; the clear sense that important masculine figures such as kings and fathers are not dispensed from—do not rightly remain aloof from or distance themselves from—participation in the messy twists and turns of the lives of those whom they purportedly love; and the notion that our care for others should extend beyond partisan categories, and indeed as widely as possible. (Along with these intellectual changes have, of course, come various alterations of human behavior and dispositions.) The first and second of the changes mentioned have had a lot to do with the diminishment of sexism and authoritarianism, and the third reflects the universalizing tendencies which were linked to moral development in previous chapters. No doubt other cultural forces are implicated as well, but moral evolution is front and center.

If you're looking for relevant "subtractions" they would certainly include these: ignorance of relational love's importance or a tendency to minimize it; a shrinking from involvement in the concrete details of others' lives, especially among men (this, of course, includes the aforementioned aloofness and distance); and adherence to arbitrary divisions, perhaps tied to authority structures, that narrow the sphere of one's concern for others. Making the God connection, we may now add that if we've subtracted these things from our conception of personal goodness, realizing that they reflect moral immaturity, we should make sure that our conception of *God's* goodness bears no traces of them. To the extent that it once did, we will see an aspect of the evolution of the God idea discussed in the previous chapter. And so if we once thought of God as Father and of God's other-regarding goodness as consisting of benevolence alone, which God extends to some creatures but not others, and which is all we need to take into account when thinking of God's "love," we will experience a shift in our thinking. We'll take on board the notion that God would have to be aware of the great value of loving relationship, and would not be closed to relationship with any persons whom God loves—a circle that would have to include everyone, unrestrictedly.

Now, there *is* a *connection* between benevolence and relational love. For the former will often provide a reason to promote the latter. Certainly it will in the divine case. This is because God, if an unspeakably rich and deep and beautiful reality, could do rather a lot to enhance the lives of others by making it possible for them to participate, to some extent, in a relationship with God. This already will give anyone attuned to what we today must regard as God's concern for the good of all a reason to say that God's moral nature, God's goodness, would include such openness toward everyone. But it is an important insight that relational love is also *intrinsically* valuable and so is rightly valued for its own sake by those who have it. If you admirably love your friend and want to continue in a relationship with him, is it just because of the good you can gain from him—or (in a kind of benevolent narcissism) hope to confer on him? No, in any deep relationship, one values what is going on for its own sake, and this even if it's also doing someone some good. So relational love, in the case of God, wouldn't just be an offshoot of benevolence. It has an independent source of value too. We therefore also have this second reason to say that a morally perfect being would display it.

Perhaps you will wonder how much value there could be for us in a relationship with God, citing the psychological gap between finite beings and their infinite creator. What could beings like us and God have in common? Well, what does an infant have in common with its adult mother? The gap *here* doesn't prevent psychological closeness of another sort: it doesn't prevent the mother from communicating affection and comfort and affording emotional security, or from delighting in each small step forward and promoting larger steps as the child grows, which also enlarges the circle of its relationships. And it doesn't prevent the child from being able to respond positively to its mother in a myriad of ways and through each response deepen and enrich the connection it has and feels to her. This point could be developed in a myriad of ways, and I suppose the analogy to the God case will be clear.

Putting the argument together

Would not be closed. . . . In my way of developing the argument, this simple subtraction does most of the work; "open" in the argument means no more than "not closed." And so after noting that

1   God would be perfectly loving,

the connection between moral evolution and a proper conception of God permits us to add

2   A perfectly loving God would always be open to relationship with everyone.

And (2) together with (1) leads us to the first conclusion of the hiddenness argument:

3 *God* would always be open to relationship with everyone.

If you're wondering why this back and forth between "a perfectly loving God" and "God," it's because the argument aims ultimately not just to show that a perfectly loving God does not exist. By means of that it aims to show that *God* does not exist.

So what exactly does (3) mean? It's important to see just how little is required by that word "open." If A is open to relationship with B, A doesn't have to be a huge extrovert who can't live without the interaction with B that such relationship involves; loving people can—like Darwin—be quite introverted and happy with solitude. But there will be a willingness to share of oneself. Even introverts, if loving, won't shut this down. For example, if A is open to a loving relationship with B, then A won't prevent B from asking A for advice, receiving encouragement from A in times of trouble, or just knowing that A is there and cares for her. A won't close herself off from B in these respects. We can get a better sense of what (3) means just by reflecting on simple undemanding facts like these.

But, you may say, God isn't a physical being who can talk to me or put an arm around my shoulder when I'm in distress. Yes, that's right. And so we'd expect the mode of any relationship with creatures like us to which God was open—the way it was maintained—to be different. Religious people know about this issue, and provide the concept of *religious experience* for us to use when dealing with it. Even if God would be a purely spiritual reality, God could give us spiritual receptors and provide a sense of the divine presence. And quite apart from religious experience, just by knowing God was there you could receive encouragement and think about your life in a whole new light, responding to God with a love of your own if you chose to do so.

But, you may wonder, wouldn't it be rather overwhelming to feel God's presence? We certainly shouldn't expect God to force such a relationship on us. Perfectly correct. That's why all I've said so far is that God would be *open* to personal relationship. This means, among other things, that we haven't at all ruled out that it would be up to created persons whether to respond with welcoming love or rather to resist a relationship with God. And as for the experience of God's presence, there's no reason to suppose that it would be all-or-nothing. The quality of God's presence, should this be felt by created persons, might change and grow as they do; it could often be a background sense—the sort of thing I experience when, writing in one room, I am peripherally aware of my wife painting in another. It could take different forms depending on the needs of the moment. It wouldn't need to be all light and roses; perhaps a relationship with a perfect God would be quite demanding in certain ways—liable to draw the best from created persons—even if never demeaning. The sense of God's presence could also be withdrawn if finite persons became too presumptuous, though, of course, without removing awareness of God and the possibility of a more suitable response on their part.

Maybe you'll still have your doubts about (2), and thus about (3). For mightn't there sometimes be special reasons for a loving God to restrict access to the divine? I think we should grant that something along these lines is true of love in human cases. One thinks here of situations like that of the young mother, still a child herself, who gives up her loved baby for adoption, and decides not to pursue a relationship with him. But it seems pretty clear, given that we've subtracted both the minimizing of the value of relationship and any shrinking from participation in it, that at a minimum the following principle is applicable here: *an admirable lover will remain open to conscious relationship whenever she has the resources to deal with the consequences of doing so, making them compatible with the flourishing of both parties and of any relationship that may come to exist between them.* Think about this principle for a bit, and you'll see that it's just spelling out something quite basic that has to go with a worthy love. And an all-knowing, all-capable God evidently would have such resources as are mentioned by the principle. So we have good reason to accept (2).

Now, as I've hinted a time or two, it's impossible for you to be related to God in the way we've been talking about without believing that God exists. Remember what I said earlier about God being able to give us spiritual receptors and provide a sense of the divine presence? About how, quite apart from religious experience, just by knowing God was there you could receive encouragement and think about your life in a whole new light? About how you might respond to God with a love of your own if you chose to do so? These are the kinds of thing in which such a relationship *consists.* And they obviously entail believing that there is a God. Without believing in God you can't think of yourself as praying to God and expect to be heard; you can't feel God's presence, identifying it as such; you can't try to find God's will for your life or experience God's forgiveness. Now, you can do other, seemingly similar things, such as praying without any expectation of being heard, perhaps motivated by hope that there is a God and that God will someday respond. But to be in a conscious relationship with God *now,* with all that alone brings, you'd need *now* to believe that God exists. It follows that preventing created beings from at some time even being aware that there is a God is a pretty good way for God to then be closed to such relationship with them. So God would never do that.

These new insights allow us to add another premise to the argument:

4   No one can be open to relationship with someone while preventing them from believing in their existence.

And from (3) and (4) together we can generate its second conclusion:

5   God would never prevent anyone from believing in God's
    existence.

To understand where the argument goes from here, let's think a bit about what it takes for you to believe in God. You can't come up with this belief or keep it going yourself, just by trying to. Believing isn't like that. *Saying* the words "God exists" is like that (singing them is too); you could *act as though* that proposition is true, just by trying to. In the same way, you could work over a period of time to *get yourself into* a believing condition by manipulating evidence. But none of this amounts to continuously believing through your own effort. If belief threatened to fail for a moment, you couldn't keep it going or bring it back, just at the drop of a hat. (If you don't believe this, you might experience a change of mind by trying to believe it—go ahead, try!) To believe something at some time, the world must seem to stand behind it, to support it, in such a way that you have the sense that it is true. As philosophers put it, belief is involuntary.

What this simple fact about belief means is that for you to believe that God exists over some period of time, the world needs to appear to stand behind God's existence through all that time. But this it won't do unless God, the world's creator, sees to it that it does. In other words, God has to *give you* the belief that God exists. Take a good close look at what will happen if God at some time drops the ball and stops supporting your belief in God. Being omniscient, God would have known ahead of time that if God did nothing, you would then fail to believe, and being omnipotent, God could easily have ensured that you kept on believing. So by doing nothing, God is knowingly making it impossible for you then to believe. And there's a pretty clear connection between "making it impossible" and "preventing"! The upshot appears to be this: if at any time someone's circumstances were as described and that person failed to believe in God's existence, God would then be preventing them from believing in God's existence—and (5) says this won't ever happen.

But one qualification we should add. A bit earlier I mentioned that I wasn't ruling out resistance to God on the part of created persons. And such resistance could lead someone to lose the belief in God that God gave him through some fault of his own—for example, by, over time, deceiving himself into thinking that the evidence for God he has been given isn't really all that great. In other words, we might, by having previously resisted God in a relevant way, at some time be preventing *ourselves* from believing in God. Should God see to it that this never happens? Presumably not, because of the value of our freedom, which is itself something love seeks to preserve.

In any case, we should say that if the cause of our nonbelief is our resistance of God, then it's not God who's preventing our belief: *we* are. So we can't say that, for any time at all, if God didn't ensure that we then believed, God would be preventing it. Maybe we'd be preventing it then, with God allowing us to do so. But just as clearly, if we aren't preventing it ourselves and still fail to believe, then we have every reason to say that God *is* preventing it. So even if we can't say that *at just any time*, if a person failed to believe in God, God would then be preventing them from believing in God, we can say the following, which builds in the needed qualification:

6 If at any time someone failed to believe in God's existence without the cause being their own resistance of God, God would then be preventing them from believing in God's existence.

Let's call the condition of believing there's no God when that's caused by your own resistance of God *resistant nonbelief*. Then from (6) together with (5) we can generate the conclusion:

7   God would never permit anyone to be a nonbeliever who was not a resistant nonbeliever.

Recognizing that someone who is not a resistant nonbeliever could be called a *nonresistant* nonbeliever, and adopting the if-then form logicians and philosophers often use, which lends itself to crisp deductive reasoning, we can turn (7) into

8   If God existed, then there would be no nonresistant nonbelief.

This is a substantial development. Indeed, with the various moves made so far, approved by careful thought and reasoning and based on insights drawn from moral evolution, the materials required for a new and powerful argument against the actual existence of God are in place. For in the actual world there is rather a lot of nonresistant nonbelief. This gives us the argument's last premise:

9   There is nonresistant nonbelief.

You see it not only in the honest doubt of many who seek for God but also in all those from earlier stages of human evolution, tens of thousands of years before theistic religions like Christianity came on the scene, who didn't believe in God because they didn't so much as have the idea of an all-powerful, all-knowing, all-good personal God, or believed in other things instead, which seemed as obvious to them as God seems to many today. If theological ignorance is the cause of your not believing in God, then resistance is *not* the cause, and so the nonbelief of these people who lived, as it were, before doubt, is a clear example of nonresistant nonbelief.

For help in its identification we are indebted to the evolutionary sciences. And so in this way cultural evolution is once again giving us a hand. But its moral dimension comes into play again too, as we think of all the nonresistant nonbelief that exists around us in the world today, so to speak *after* doubt. Here we can apply some points first raised in Chapter 1: that we will accept that much nonbelief is honest, caused by genuine bewilderment as to the truth of the matter and serious questions about the evidence rather than resistance of God, because we have learned to empathize with those who tell us of their doubts, and, having ourselves been exposed to religious diversity and the power of secularity, are able to see that oftentimes nonbelief is not corrupt, contrary to what believers before the moral evolution of which I've spoken generally quite breezily assumed.

The long and the short of it is that we today have plenty of reason to accept (9). But now look at what follows from (8) and (9), taken together:

10   God does not exist.

The argument here—the hiddenness argument—could be stated more loosely and succinctly as follows. If God existed, there wouldn't be any nonresistant nonbelief. But there is nonresistant nonbelief. So God does not exist. Both premises, notice, are brought to mind and made supportable by cultural evolution. The reasoning here has exactly the same form as the following simple example: If John lost the race, then he didn't come first. But he did come first. So he didn't lose the race. If you can see why, in this simple example, you have to accept that John didn't lose the race, you will be able to see why we have to accept the conclusion of the preceding argument, that God does not exist, if we accept its premises. Another way of putting our result here is to say that our world contains something—nonresistant nonbelief—that it wouldn't contain had God created it. So no God created our world. But if God existed, God *would* have created our world. So God doesn't exist.

Just by thinking through, then, what moral evolution means for our conception of God—in this case, by thinking through the nature of relational love—we stumble on a new way of arguing that there is no God. The hiddenness argument has been receiving a lot of discussion among philosophers lately, who feel its force, and I'm pretty sure this is because philosophers, like anyone else, bear in their psyches the marks of cultural change. That these changes include recent developments like feminism and the receding of authoritarian governments and class distinctions may furthermore help to explain why it is only now that this argument is being discussed, in the midst of a discussion—the Western discussion about God—that is more than 2,000 years old.

7

A Kinder God

The hiddenness argument is relatively new. The argument from evil against the existence of God, by contrast, has been with us for a very long time. Even the old God displayed benevolence, with or without relational love, and however fitfully or partially, and thoughtful people throughout the history of theism have wondered how such a God's existence is to be squared with the existence of bad things like the vast suffering unleashed by a tsunami or the wickedness of a Hitler. This problem, as noted a couple of chapters ago, was the problem for theism that most impressed and influenced Darwin. The theologian Hans Küng has called it the "rock of atheism."

So what occasion or need is there for something new in this neighborhood? As it happens, the problem of evil is considerably sharpened when we take moral evolution into account, in connection with the very worst cases of suffering the world has seen, which we may call *horrors*. Since this problem is already agreed on (virtually) all hands to be very serious, an obvious *worsening* of the problem might be expected to render it insoluble—at least by theists. In such circumstances, the rock of atheism might become immovable.

To their credit, philosophers who defend the idea of God's existence in the face of the suffering this world contains generally don't try to sugarcoat the truth about how bad things can get. Rather, they try to bring out very clearly the truly horrifying features of so much pain and anguish that human beings and nonhuman animals suffer and have suffered on planet Earth. Thus you find Alvin Plantinga relating the true story of a man who accidentally crushes his own small child under the wheels of his big truck as he backs off the driveway after lunch. And Marilyn McCord Adams describes how a woman was raped and had her arms hacked off with an axe. This too actually happened. Adams calls such events *horrendous*, defining horrendous suffering as suffering that gives surviving victims or (as the case may be) perpetrators a reason—not necessarily a conclusive reason, but a reason—to think that their lives are not worth living. I myself, as suggested before, am calling such events horrors. Regardless of the label, it's clear that some cases of suffering are more dreadful than others in the way Adams suggests, and that the most extreme are mind-bendingly, stupefyingly horrible.

So this is the class of evils on which we'll be focusing. Moral evolution, as I'll now show, makes the case for atheism that can be constructed from it even more forceful than has generally been supposed, and arguably decisive.

Divine empathy

Among the evolutionary "subtractions" we've mentioned are partial and arbitrarily discriminating care, callous indifference, uncaring and unsympathetic tendencies, and resigned acquiescence when others suffer greatly and have their lives torn apart. Considering these carefully, one realizes that the proper religious effects of moral evolution would have to involve, at the very least, an enlarged and enriched sense of how immensely seriously any perfectly good being would take the thought of permitting horrors to befall anyone. If not uncaring and unkind about such things, God obviously must be caring and kind, and in the deepest and best possible way. To capture the central idea here, we might speak of a maximally deep and sensitive and kindly *concern* being evoked by the thought of horrors. (It might seem natural to speak of compassion instead, but compassion is evoked by actual suffering, and the argument I'm developing begins from a point prior to any suffering being permitted, when the possibility of not permitting it remains.)

Another subtraction we've noted is a willingness to remain distant from the feelings of others. If we excise this from our conception of God too, we have the result that God would be unwilling to remain distant and so would be found drawing close to the feelings of other beings, gaining a sense of how they feel or "feeling with" them instead. It's natural to call this the divine *empathy* if—as I will—we assume that it's motivated by the kindly concern just mentioned. In the previous chapter we saw how the new God would be willing to come close to any created persons there might be, out of relational love. That insight generated the hiddenness argument. But there's also this other way of "coming close" involving empathy.

Morally sensitive people today are keenly aware of the value of empathy in a well-formed moral personality. Steven Pinker reminds us that it was not always recognized as being so important, at least not in the West. Various events had to occur for things to evolve in its direction. Pinker interestingly suggests that one of them was a sharp increase in novel reading starting in the late eighteenth century: reading a novel puts you into the minds of its characters, and forces you to experience their lives with them in ways that can make you better at "feeling with"—empathizing with—conscious beings in the real world too. Now, empathy can go off the rails if the sense one has of others' feelings is in some way mistaken, and it can be unbalanced by other values, leading one to go easier on the person with whom one empathizes than one should. But even after due acknowledgment of such points, we are left with the following: empathizing with other people or even with nonhuman animals such as horses or cats in ways we should, we are less likely to see them as so different from ourselves as to allow us to treat them as we wouldn't ever treat ourselves, with casual violence or in other insensitive ways.

After the moral evolution that has brought us to this point, it's easy for us to see that God would be *unsurpassably* empathetic. This means that a God would have the deepest possible empathy and employ it in the best possible ways. Notice now that to do so God would have to be able to be aware of just what it would be like, from the inside, to be this or that created being in this or that situation in which they might be placed. Let's now have a closer look at this awareness.

As the word suggests, this awareness would be a form of knowledge, and so just by reflecting on the thought that God would be omniscient, or all-knowing, we can see that we have to attribute to God the capacity for such awareness. (Here as a side benefit of our deepened understanding of God's goodness we get a deepened understanding of God's knowledge.) Philosophers have often analyzed omniscience in a purely "external" way, as involving the best possible access to propositional truths, such as the truth that $2 + 2 = 4$. God on this view is like the greatest possible scientist, who knows the solutions to all scientific problems and can answer any question you might put to him. But the new idea of God will have more in it than this—with the more adequate understanding of omniscience our evolution allows, we'll say that God would not just know that conscious beings exist, if they do, and are put together in such and such a way within the structures provided by their environment but also would know what it *feels* like, from the inside, to be a conscious creature of this or that sort.

How could a God have this access? We already know something of what it is to have access to the feelings of another, and of what it is to have it improved, from our own experience of such things. So one way to start conceiving God's access would involve imagining an indefinite *extension* of the improvements we ourselves have managed in any particular case. As much knowledge as can thus be acquired an unlimited God would have to be able to have. But being the creator of any finite beings there may be and all-powerful, God would presumably have a readier access than that to the inner life of any possible conscious being, including persons. Even if God couldn't literally have another person's experiences, qualitatively identical experiences would be on tap, which give God what philosophers call "knowledge by acquaintance" of any possible person's inner life, and in particular of their suffering. We would do justice to neither the divine power nor the divine goodness if we said otherwise.

Empathy and horrors

So it is with such knowledge and with the unsurpassable empathy it informs that we have to imagine a divine creator approaching the thought of producing finite persons and letting them suffer horrifically. For universe creation to be a responsible act, one would *have* to know what one was doing, considering it most carefully. And thus *God* would have to know, and would have to know in our enriched sense which includes feeling what it would be like, from the inside, to experience horrors. Given this fact, could God realize that such horrors might very well befall certain possible persons in the circumstances in which God is thinking of actualizing them—but actualize them in those circumstances anyway?

One perhaps tempting move just says *no*. This move doesn't even get as far as giving an argument, with premises and conclusions. It just asks you to try to conceive the following situation: a being as empathetic as God would be becomes intimately acquainted with our world, as a candidate for creation, with the most vivid and detailed knowledge feeling the terror of a child slowly suffocating underground after an earthquake and the excruciating and degrading pain of the woman who is raped and has her limbs hacked off, as well as the inner reality of countless similar events, and then says, "Yes, let's have *that* world!" You can't do it—not without swiftly transforming the imagined being in your mind into, if not a sadistic monster, then at least a being restricted to an external standpoint, without any real or vivid awareness of what the inner lives of the creatures whose existence is being contemplated are like. In other words, it's quite impossible that an unsurpassably empathetic God should select, for creation, a world with such horrors as our own, and we can see this without argument, much as we can just see that $2 + 2 = 4$.

That's one possible move, and it's one we may expect to have a lot of appeal after the moral evolution we've undergone. But a new argument for atheism, the argument from horrors, can be generated too. And it may in the end be convincing in a wider range of cases. To get warmed up for it, just think for a little longer about the enormity of the implications of divine empathy for the inner life and dispositions of any God there may be. In particular, think once again of what it would be like for an unsurpassably empathetic being to experience so fully all the horrific suffering of our world, held before the divine mind as a candidate for creation.

This is, of course, a mind-boggling task. But perhaps we can make a beginning in it if we think a little about the effects of somewhat similar states in human beings. Think first of people who are to some degree empathetic but not in any sense very "close" to horrors. This might describe most of us, who make do with journalists' reports or with imaginative extrapolation from our own—not very high—peaks of pain, and occasionally make some effort in the direction of relieving suffering through a donation to Oxfam or some such thing. We have "normalized" suffering to a considerable extent. (Familiarity breeds tolerance.) Even while calling it horrific, we really can hardly help not knowing—and underestimating—how bad horrific suffering truly is and having our own motivation to do something about it diluted by other concerns. In fact it's disconcerting to think of how, though we know horrors are happening around us and hear of them every day, precisely because we ourselves are alive and well and able to take in the news at our leisure, we are disqualified from really knowing what the suffering we read about is like. Everyone who's talking about it is, for the same reason, unable really to comprehend it, and so what is going on around us every day may be far more awful than we tend to imagine. The responses of those who do experience it and survive provide support for this assessment—as we'll see in a few moments.

So the task we face here isn't an easy one. But imagine next being given a shot of empathy and immediately transported from that comfortable spot in front of your TV into the heart of the human devastation left behind by a tsunami or a terrorist bombing, or think of those who actually are day by day brought close to horrific suffering in this way—journalists, doctors, and (for a seriously intensified version of empathy plus proximity to horrific suffering) the Mother Teresas and Gandhis of our world. With a little bit of empathy and as little contact with horrors as most of us have, we already will display some opposition to horrors. And with greater empathy and with greater proximity to much horrific suffering—more of a sense of what it's like to suffer in this way—comes a *stronger* opposition to such suffering, including a fuller investment of time and energy devoted to its elimination and prevention.

And now let's intensify empathy and proximity to horrific suffering one more time. In particular, let's think of those whose "proximity" to it is as great as it can be for us humans, because they have experienced such suffering *for themselves*. Of course, it's in the nature of the case that the number of such sufferers who survive and return to active life is relatively small, but some do, and from their experience and subsequent dispositions we might hope to glean the fullest glimpse of the effects of divine empathy. Now, it certainly appears from the examples that could be cited (take Elie Wiesel, the author of the well-known and disturbing little book *Night*, for one) that those who have experienced such suffering and are empathetic become very strongly and indeed unalterably opposed to its occurrence in other cases—few who suffer thus can subsequently think of very much apart from the eradication and prevention of such suffering. And, of course, the rest of us praise and admire them for their efforts.

Therefore, taking stock of these human cases, we have the first premise of our argument:

1   As a concerned human being's empathy and proximity to horrors increase, they will approach and eventually reach an absolute opposition to horrors—a disposition to seek to eliminate and prevent horrors wherever they can.

And now add what we have seen to be true about empathy in the divine case:

2   God would be *maximally* concerned and empathetic and *maximally* close to horrors that might occur in our world if it were created—maximally well acquainted from every vantage point, and in particular from the inside, with every bit of horrific suffering to be found in our world.

It may seem that we can immediately draw the conclusion that God too, and even more obviously, would be absolutely opposed to horrors and thus opposed to actualizing worlds containing horrors like ours. Instead of our world or a world like ours in this respect, so it may appear, God would create another world (if God creates at all). Does this conclusion follow?

The fact that God, unlike mere mortals, would not be psychologically overwhelmed by proximity to horrors doesn't stand in its way. For if we think of our enlarged empathy as signaling moral progress, we must say that what's doing the work here is not psychological weakness but moral acuity: specifically, a new awareness of the awfulness of horrors.

Another unsuccessful attempt to block the conclusion is this: if horrors like those found in our world were deleted, bad things at the next level, as it were, would take their place, seeming to us just as bad, so that nothing worthwhile would be gained. But this is not the case, precisely because of how bad horrors are. We've linked them with the notion of being given a reason to think that one's life is not worth living, and many bad things people experience do not give one such a reason. In any case, the thought in question seems subject to a confusion: it infers, correctly, that bad things at the next level down would now be the *worst* evils we experience and regarded as the worst, but it does not follow, as it appears to suppose, that these bad things have to be *very bad* or viewed as very bad. The worst thing you find in some context may not be very bad, just as the best need not be very good. The worst thing that happened to me last month was a mildly sprained ankle, and although it irritates me, I concede that things could be a lot worse!

So these two responses don't work. But something else may still stand in the way of that conclusion.

Offsetting goods?

Consider the following move. "Suppose that God's unsurpassable knowledge, so much greater than ours, includes not only the awareness involved in unsurpassable empathy but also the knowledge that there are very good situations that can be brought into the world only by permitting horrors to occur. The argument from horrors needs to be able to rule this out. But how could it ever do so? How can we ever be sure that there's nothing God would see as worth aiming for that brings with it the risk of horrors? To make the argument from horrors work, we'd need to add a premise about there being no good situations like that. But such a premise could never fly, given our own limitations and in particular our ignorance about the full range of goods and the possible deep connections between evils and goods."

This point is well taken—to an extent! I agree that some proposition entailing the premise mentioned here should be included in the argument. So let's add one now:

3   A maximally concerned and empathetic God who was
    maximally well acquainted with horrors could not be
    sufficiently motivated to bring about goods requiring the
    permission of horrors.

What I want to show is how in the new dispensation of theist-atheist reasoning ushered in by our recent moral progress and in particular by sensitivity to empathy, this intermediate premise proposed by the objection, which it will think we have no reason to accept and so see as a weak link in the argument's chain of reasoning, is in fact a premise we are fully justified in affirming as true.

The key is to see how unsurpassable empathy would function as a *constraint* on the sort of good situation that could possibly be good enough. Clearly, extrapolating from how empathetic people are disposed, we have to say that an unsurpassably empathetic being such as God would not easily permit horrors. Of course, that's a massive understatement. The good state of affairs would have to be at least as attractive to God as horrors are repulsive, which is to say it would have to be unbelievably, unspeakably attractive. Putting this a bit differently, the thought of that good not being made real would have to be at least as repulsive to God as the thought of permitting horrors—which is to say unbelievably, unspeakably repulsive. Putting it differently yet again, God would have to be as motivated to produce that good despite the connection to horrors as, given the combination of unsurpassable empathy and concern and unsurpassed access to horrific suffering, God would be motivated to prevent such suffering.

And here's the thing. Even if there are goods that require the permission of horrors, none could possibly rise to that level—none could possibly be motivating for an unsurpassably empathetic God in the required way—because of all the good that *doesn't* require permitting horrors that would always be available to an omniscient and omnipotent being thinking about its creative options.

Let's consider this closely. Where could horror-associated goods possibly be needed? If God would be a perfect being, then certainly *God* couldn't need anything for which permitting horrors might somehow be required. And here's the more pertinent point: given the richness of any being that displayed the wisest, loveliest, deepest possible personality and did so without evil, there would always be literally an infinite number of ways, corresponding to the infinite beauty of God, in which created beings, including personal beings, could be led into a most wondrous existence simply by being led to mimic in their own life some aspect of the unsurpassably wonderful, horror-free life of God or by being allowed to participate in a personal relationship with God. (Here we are returned to a notion central to the previous chapter.) So we can answer the objection we are contemplating by saying that reflection on the greatness of God is alone sufficient to show that there could be no goods requiring the permission of horrors that would lead an unsurpassably empathetic being to permit them.

Should we be given pause by the response sometimes suggested in these discussions: that by being forced to live with horrors, by seeking to overcome the most extreme physical and emotional challenges, human beings have a chance to show themselves at their very best—to be *heroes*? After Chapter 4 that notion of being a hero should bring to mind earlier stages of moral evolution, and in particular the one-sided emphasis on personal honor in ancient Greece which Kitcher described and showed to be superseded by an emphasis on working together as a group for common goods. For us today it should be quite clear that individual heroism in the experience of horrors is not a good that would be sufficiently motivating for an unsurpassably empathetic God. Besides, with a little imagination we can see how plenty of opportunity would remain for something rather like heroism, even if there were no horrors at all in a world created by God. In a world somewhat like ours this might mean straining every nerve to reach the highest and most useful station in one of many regions of politics, academia, business, medicine, athletics, or the arts. And what about growing out of various forms of *human immaturity*, both individually and collectively? It is so easy to neglect this difficult challenge. A great deal of heroism is called for here! In any case, heroism doesn't require horrors specifically, as distinguished from bad things that might continue to happen even if horrors were excised from God's creative plan. In fact, horrors are so bad that they rather often simply crush the human beings subjected to them, thus making quite impossible the proposed heroic response.

The additional premise we've been checking out therefore seems quite acceptable rather than vulnerable as the objection would suggest. And what follows from the three premises we have so far? Surely this conclusion:

4   If God existed, then should there be any world at all, it would have to be some other *horror-free* world rather than our world.

And the most obvious premise of all comes next:

5   Our world exists.

But from 4 and 5 we can derive the conclusion that

6   God does not exist.

Given the resources today made available to inquirers by moral evolution, the expanded—the finished—version of the argument from horrors is quite sound. The rock of atheism stands firm and secure.

8

A Nonviolent God

I grew up in the Canadian province of Manitoba, on a mostly bald prairie punctuated by evergreen windbreaks, bunches of wind-tousled poplars, and stately grain elevators, among Mennonites committed to a doctrine of nonviolence. At least most of them were. My parents retained ethnic features that went with being Mennonite but ceased to identify with "traditional" pacifist views upon being converted, in their youth, to born-again evangelicalism. Nonetheless, I was always peripherally aware of the link between being Mennonite and believing in nonviolence as a way of life.

These days the Mennonites are far from alone in praising nonviolence; as noted in Chapter 4, moral evolution has conspired to make most of us a good deal less violent than were earlier examples of *Homo sapiens*, and, of course, the Gandhis and Kings of the last century have made famous the political power of nonviolent resistance. But the nonviolence of Mennonites is still in a way distinctive, since it goes back to the Reformation of the sixteenth century and the belief of some of the more radical reformers that to know Christ one must follow him not just in word but in life, which they took to imply the cultivation, even under provocation and risk to life or limb, of gentleness rather than reactive forcefulness, respectfulness rather than harsh and demeaning rudeness, and self-sacrifice rather than selfish domination. Mennonites, like all Christians, hold that Jesus of Nazareth displayed something of the character of God, but more than most, they stress that the nonviolence of Jesus is central to this revelatory display.

Of course, this creates some notable tensions with the idea that God is the God-of-the-Bible, who clearly sanctioned war and killing rather often, at least in the Christian Old Testament. Mennonites downplay this and sometimes try to explain it away. But the idea that nonviolence is a window into the heart of God creates an even more notable— though generally unnoted—tension with the idea that God created a violent world. Indeed, one way of making a central point of this book, which I'll be elaborating here, is to say that if Mennonites were perfectly consistent, they would be led to atheism, as the realization that a nonviolent God would not have created *this* world hits home.

huh ? (margin note)

The problem of violence

The problem here may seem quite similar to the one discussed in the previous chapter. But while violence and pain or suffering are often causally linked, the corresponding notions are conceptually quite distinct. Notice first how pain and suffering can occur without violence. Worlds are imaginable in which the natural state involves the most dreadful suffering from the beginning to the end of life, without violent acts or events being needed to bring it about. Even in the actual world the agonizing pain of certain diseases approaches slowly and gently.

Now turn that around. It's also the case that violence can occur— and be bad—without pain or suffering. This is less obvious, but to see it, it will help to have before us what I have in mind in this chapter when I speak of violence. I have in mind *sensitive beings made subject* to harsh and rude force rather than gentleness and respect. It's precisely the badness of this feature of violence, so I suggest, its violation of creaturely dignity, that our moral progress has made obvious to us. And it would be bad even if no pain or suffering came with it. Moreover, it would be bad even without the other thing with which the badness of violence is sometimes wrongly conflated: the abrupt ending of valuable lives.

We need an example. Here's one: if the blunt impact of a hammer wielded in anger causes for your cat or dog or even your young child an immediate but temporary loss of consciousness, during which its effects are repaired, a living being is treated with rude force without ever on its account experiencing pain or suffering or having its life shortened. There's no pain or suffering or shortened life to complain about here. But notice that we would or should object to what happened here nonetheless.

It follows, then, from what we've seen so far that what's objectionable according to the argument from violence to be developed in this chapter is not the same as what we were talking about in the previous chapter or indeed what's being talked about in pretty much any discussion of the problem of evil. It's a problem in its own right, which moral evolution has exposed.

A key fact here is, of course, that human beings, and in their own ways many other organisms too, are exquisitely complex and sophisticated entities, often with a perspective on the world and accompanying beliefs, desires, and purposes. Violence toward such beings was once much more common among us, and even today we often take it for granted. But more and more we are coming to sense how immensely bad is the violent treatment of such a valuable entity, with its rich inner life and—where the perspective on the world is joined to memory and anticipation and guided by reason—a life-narrative sheltering hopes and dreams.

Something other than "disutility" or a loss of well-being is at stake here. The harsh interruption of a life violates its dignity; it is completely contrary to the gentleness with which such complex, intricately structured, sensitive beings deserve to be treated. Take, for example, George Orwell's autobiographical story, *Shooting an Elephant,* in which an Indian coolie is minding his business when an elephant comes around the corner and crushes him with its foot, leaving him sunk in the mud with a sharply twisted head: "His face was coated with mud, the eyes wide open, the teeth bared and grinning." And we should not ignore the violence done to the elephant later in the story, which suddenly meets its end in a rain of bullets while chewing grass. Again, although these examples involve death, what I'll be focused on in this chapter would be present even if we were to delete that part: the coolie's dignity is violated when his thinking is so rudely and harshly interrupted, and so is the elephant's when while chewing grass he is suddenly hurled to the ground.

As we've already started to see, there are different kinds of violence. But all would have to have been ordained or permitted by God if this were God's world. Paradigmatically, we see violence in certain human behaviors and dispositions. But if we take the term fairly broadly, as seems appropriate given our purposes, then it can also be seen in certain behaviors and dispositions of other animals (a lion's way of tearing apart a gazelle is violent—and, of course, Orwell's coolie-crushing elephant is apropos). Moreover, violence appears in analogously harsh natural events such as species-decimating asteroid impacts or a suddenly disabling lightning strike. Let's call these human violence, animal violence, and natural violence, respectively. Obviously the categories overlap somewhat, and much in them may even be reducible to the operation of one or another common factor such as Darwinian natural selection. Equally obviously, although human violence may slowly be abating, there is still a lot of it around, mixed in with the sedate and the wondrous in life. Multiple examples populate every minute.

And so it has been *for millions of years*. Here once again we see how biological evolution comes into the picture secondarily. Nature was red in tooth and claw for a long, long time before human hands and human tools came along to wreak their own distinctive brand of havoc. And from the advent of sentient life natural disasters too have threatened violence, often enough following through on the threat. Of course, this isn't all we see; the world is far from unmitigatedly bad. But for the badness of its plentiful violence a creator God would bear the responsibility, if there were such a being.

So what should be our response to the thought of a God who sanctions violence, after the moral evolution we've been going through and a commensurate evolution in our religious views? I think we need to face the fact that a God whose character displayed to fullest effect what we have learned about the moral magnificence of nonviolence would never behave in this way. If we mentally push the idea of God as a perfect personal being through the history of moral evolution, gathering new insights into our conception of God's goodness as we go, it may come to seem rather clear that, given a world suffused with violence, there is no God. Learning from what I've said about the Mennonites specifically, we should ask how, if we value gentleness and respect and so think of these qualities as unsurpassably exemplified in God, we can ever imagine God ordaining or permitting processes which have the result that for millions of years animals rudely tear each other to shreds and natural forces harshly exert a similarly rude, crushing, and demeaning force, so opposed to the dignity of complex living beings.

Someone meditating on such considerations will feel the force of a new atheistic argument that starts out like this:

1   There is far more violence in our world than is compatible with the existence of a nonviolent God.

The argument continues by noting, as our moral progress should lead us to say, that

2 God would be nonviolent.

But from (1) and (2) it follows that

3 If God existed, then should there be any world at all, it would be some world other than our violent world.

Again, the most obvious premise is about the existence of the world:

4 Our violent world exists.

And from (3) and (4) together we have our final conclusion that

5 God does not exist.

Of course, religious conviction may protest against such a conclusion, but what will we say if we recall, from Chapter 1, philosophy's passionate indifference?

Some possible solutions

Precisely with that attitude, a theist may now say, we need to investigate possible *solutions* of the problem this argument presents for belief in God, such as the one appealing to free will. Indeed, it is quite commonly held that human violence can be chalked up to our own free will rather than to anything that a creator would be morally responsible for. The apparent availability of such a move is likely to leave many theists quite sanguine about the problem of violence—and in particular about the chances of successfully resisting premise 1 of the above argument.

But this move is vulnerable to defeat. Leaving aside for now that human behavior in its entirety is just one startlingly brief episode in the history of sentient life's exposure to violence, let me identify three worries.

First, it is not at all obvious that we even have free will of the sort required here. Sure, we often make choices quite spontaneously and with malice aforethought, but it is an open possibility—with every success of the social sciences a more widely open one—that all our choices and thoughts, along with everything else going on in and around us (including our impulse to blame people for nasty things they appear to have freely done!), are part of a huge and complex natural web in which everything is caused by something else. In the more cold and abstract language of philosophy, it's possible that *determinism* is true.

But suppose we have the required sort of free will. Much human violence happens when, as it were, our free will is shut off. Even believers in free will have to grant that there are rather frequent occasions when because of environmental or genetic influence or both, human beings are simply overwhelmed by violent tendencies, harshly lashing out at others or themselves. In such cases, how could we be said to be morally responsible for human violence?

And this point leads us swiftly to the third worry. This is that even if we are often violent because we exercise free will violently, it's only because of more basic dispositions of anger, bitterness, resentfulness, jealousy, rudeness, and so on, which are deeply woven into our nature. Without those dispositions, you would never think to lift a finger or word against anyone. Pretty clearly, even if some humans learn to diminish or counteract the power of such tendencies and use their free will to do so, that any human being has them in the first place is not something for which we're morally responsible. These are things for which God would be morally responsible, if God had created this world. Here we bump into a point at once rather obvious and apparently quite easy to forget. This is that if there is free will in a world created by God, it can only be because *God wants it there*. God would therefore have to be indirectly morally responsible for any violence issuing from free will and for whatever lies behind it, making it possible, in the same way that you'd be responsible if you created a robot with destructive impulses and set it loose in your neighborhood.

So a God would be morally responsible for violence. But that realization only prepares us for a more sophisticated kind of solution which is compatible with this observation—which hopes to provide good reasons for even a perfectly good and thus a nonviolently disposed creator to ordain or permit the violence on our planet, reasons which might allow us to reject the argument's first premise. Though the argument from violence does not explicitly appear in the literature—a sign that atheists have not been attending to the consequences of moral evolution—the makings of two reasons can be detected here and there in what has been written about the problem of evil. I will identify these reasons and then show why they lack force. As I do, the distinctive resources made available by the new evolutionary approach will again be coming into play.

The first reason goes back to free will, trying to come up with a one-size-fits-all response. It argues (a) that it would be a very good thing for finite created persons to be given significant free will involving the power to behave violently or to refrain from doing so, (b) that the full sweep of the evolutionary story as revealed by science, which includes much violence, really represents the only arena in which free creatures like us could come to be, and moreover (c) that an evolutionary world with such violence is a *highly appropriate* space for the exercise of creaturely freedom.

Let's very briefly expand on these points, one at a time. (a) Free will is valuable both because of the inherent dignity autonomy affords and because it is needed for what John Hick, borrowing from John Donne, has called "soul-making": being able through our own serious and consequential choices, whether for good or ill, to become the beings we choose to be. (b) A long evolutionary road is required to reach rational beings like us who are able to understand the consequences of their choices, organically sophisticated creatures with free will. (c) In an evolutionary world, we constantly are able, through our choices, to promote progress toward higher things or else permit regression. Indeed, as Richard Swinburne has suggested, a God who molded such creatures would be setting them in a half-finished world and making them in effect cocreators, affording them the wonderful opportunity to participate in the production of the finished world that finally will be.

I have developed this reason for permitting violence as charitably as I could. And it certainly does have some attractions. Notice, for example, how the emphasis on dignity and responsibility can be seen as cutting against the demeaning aspects of evolutionary violence. But it is nonetheless not a very good or strong reason to suppose that God, as understood in the light of moral and religious evolution, would permit the violence our world contains, and this even if we accept the dubious idea that we have free will of the sort required. Indeed, even if we accept that we have free will and accept all of the points gathered under (a), (b), and (c), we still should deny that it is a good reason. This is because one way of getting something, whether valuable freedom, or rational organic beings, or an arena suitable to the exercise of free will, is here repeatedly and mistakenly assumed to be the *only* way. And this won't do, given that a good reason for God to permit violence would have to show not only that violence can be conducive to good things such as free will but also that God can't get those good things in any other way. If God could get them in another way, then we no more have an excuse for God to permit violence than a superpowered dentist who can fix your teeth by snapping his fingers has an excuse for drilling into them and fixing them in the slow and painful old-fashioned way.

But why should serious thinkers make such an elementary error, confusing what's sufficient with what's necessary? Many of them, I surmise, do not see the error because they are thinking outward from us, instead of inward from God: the reasoner we are considering thinks only about what's needed to get free beings *like us*, evolved physical and organic beings. Even then, arguably, there is a mistake, since an omnipotent God presumably could realize something like the scenario of Genesis 1 and 2 in the Bible literally interpreted, with organic beings that are "readymade" rather than evolved.

Starting from thoughts about God and God's creative options instead, we would, for example, notice immediately that God would not be a physical evolved being, and so we would be led to the thought that the creation of finite and free personal beings who are not evolved or even physical would (given omnipotence) be possible for God and also (given the violence of the alternative) be preferable. There would be plenty of scope for serious and responsible choices for created finite beings in a nonviolent and nonphysical world. Mythical tales of heavens and hells as well as some regions of science fiction can help our imaginations assure us of this. Indeed, even without possibilities of harm, ways of being significantly free will become visible if we think carefully enough about the nature of God. For example, if God is the deepest, greatest, most fascinatingly rich personal being possible, there would always be new dimensions of God or of God's creations or of God's projects to get to know or to participate in, and corresponding choices—even difficult and demanding choices— to be made. Sure, we're most familiar with our own mode of being and so are naturally drawn to it, but if we want the truth instead of comfortable familiarity we should swallow hard and admit that there'd be no reason for God to be creatively biased in favor of us! And once we let that thought go, it won't be hard to see how a nonviolent God would be led in a different direction. We, of course, would prefer a world in which we exist, but *our* perspective *now* is one thing, and God's before all creation quite another.

But I said there are two reasons for violence we can imagine a theist coming up with. What is the second reason? It is an *aesthetic* reason. Think of the aesthetic value of drama, someone might say, which is heightened by the intensity of conflict, particularly conflict between good and evil. Of course, there could still be conflict of a sort without violence, but a world with no violence would have radically less in the way of dramatic value. And there is another kind of aesthetic value in the spare elegance and simplicity of a physical universe governed by a few regularities expressible as mathematical equations. God couldn't get this kind of value and also continually step in to prevent violence from occurring. Finally, there is aesthetic value in the evolutionary process itself to which even Darwin testified as he concluded his great book *On the Origin of Species*:

> There is grandeur in this view of life, with its several powers, having been originally breathed into a few forms or into one; and that, whilst this planet has gone cycling on according to the fixed law of gravity, from so simple a beginning endless forms most beautiful and wonderful have been, and are being evolved.

However, as we know, the grandeur of the evolutionary process comes at the cost of much natural violence.

Now, it may seem that aesthetic value of these kinds couldn't possibly outweigh the moral disvalue associated with aeons of violence. But to make this aesthetic reason as forceful as it can be, we might note a couple of things: (i) that cultural evolution has recently brought us, if anything, more aesthetic sensitivity and more awareness of the diversity of value than we had before, and (ii) that being, as I have argued, in various ways immature, the species might still not properly appreciate how very great aesthetic value of the kinds in question would be. So this should leave us open to the possibility that God would make the value judgments required to tolerate a world as violent as ours.

Is the aesthetic reason for promoting or tolerating violence sufficiently forceful? I don't think so. Here's why. You can take the aesthetic value of violence-infused drama, of simple and elegant laws of nature, and of certain structural features of the evolutionary process to be as great as you like, but still if you accept this way of thinking as forceful you will be making basically the same mistake we had before, in connection with the first reason: treating something that is *sufficient* for the production of value—in this case, aesthetic value—as though it were *necessary*. This is easy to do. We easily think of violence as being necessary for certain things like drama when it's really only necessary for the forms of those things that we know best. Our limited imaginations don't help: it's easy to think that if violence is rejected, we must be ready to settle for the bland and the boring, when we really should be thinking of this constraint as an invitation to more daring intellectual expeditions.

As it happens, some of the things with which we're quite familiar themselves compete very well with the violence-fed ways of realizing aesthetic value we have contemplated. There is much grandeur in the work of Handel and Mozart. And a lot of drama in Beethoven! All three composers come to us without actual violence. So imagine that a nonviolent spiritual universe were designed to be like a glorious piece of music writ large, except with God as the Composer, and that finite persons were given a taste for aesthetics or the ability to cultivate it, and able to traverse the wonders of this universe, or even with extreme exertion to enlarge upon them, forever or for a finite period of time. And, of course, such a "universe" would in a way already exist in the violence-free being of God, without any need to create something new. Just as we've noted before, finite beings could be given the opportunity to get to know this "universe"—an activity that, given their finitude and God's rich infinities, could be indefinitely prolonged and realized in endless varieties, each more wondrous than the last. Why should we suppose that anything is missing here which only *violence* could supply? Why suppose that a nonviolent God would ever look longingly over the fence at violent worlds, finding appealing the crushing of sensitive bodies and minds, when aesthetic value in endless forms most beautiful and wonderful could otherwise be generated?

You may reply that a violent world like ours affords extra aesthetic value—and aesthetic value of a distinctive kind. Seeing it, after considering what might otherwise be made available, we'll naturally say: "Look, there's more!" But two points taken together with this one remove any force it may appear to have. First, infinity is infinity: wherever one may pause in an elaboration of divine aesthetic value— wherever God might pause—and quite without turning to violence-based aesthetics, one would *always* be able to say: "Look, there's more!" Second, what makes violence-based aesthetic value distinctive also contributes a distinctive and deep *badness*. This was once easy to miss, but our own moral progress now makes it known unto us. A God, who would always and unsurpassably exemplify what we have laboriously learned about the moral importance of nonviolence, should not be expected to miss it.

Here again—just as in the last chapter—we see how much more powerfully positioned is the atheist who leaves behind anti-God confusion, working rather with an approach that is pro-God, in the sense that it emphasizes how amazing a divine reality would have to be. For one thing, only when facing in this direction can we even see the relevance of human moral evolution and moral progress to discussion of the divine. But as noted several times in these chapters in which we've been developing some of the arguments of a new and progressive atheism, we also encounter a more specific relevance when various goods are put forward by theists to try to solve problems like those we've developed. For they all are swamped by the immeasurably greater good that would have to be realized in God.

* * *

There may well be yet other ways of arguing in the same rich vein I've been mining in this and the previous two chapters, and other ways of responding. The arguments I've elaborated are only meant to be illustrative. Even so, a new method for atheistic inquiry is here emerging: consider how cultural evolution has changed our thinking, especially around morality, and search the results for premises that might today support atheism even if at one time they would have gone unnoticed or been ignored. With the emergence of this method, we see the possibility of a distinctive approach to atheism, more powerful than those that came before. As noted, I'm calling it *progressive* atheism. But there are some reasons for regarding this approach as superior to those that came before, and for calling it progressive, that we have yet to consider.

9

Challenging the New Theism

Progressive atheism, as we've just seen, has some powerful new arguments, grounded in human moral progress, which anyone can use to reason in defense of the conclusion that God does not exist. These already enable a further kind of progress—progress *for atheism*. But progressive atheism is also poised to support progress in certain more specific ways which I want to take up in the book's two concluding chapters. The first way, which I'll consider in this chapter, takes us to a more specific sort of progress for atheism in relation to theistic philosophy. Theistic philosophy has seen a remarkable resurgence recently but, due to the circumstances of the cultural moment we're presently in, has yet to be forcefully and effectively engaged. Progressive atheism looks ready and able to take it on.

Rise of the new theism

The Presocratic Anaxagoras, in his quasi-theistic ruminations on Mind as an independent feature of reality, started a discussion that was to long continue among Western philosophers, especially after a lot of Christians and other theists joined their ranks in the early centuries of the Common Era. There then followed a relatively dry period for theistic philosophy linked to the Enlightenment and the rise of science. But recently, to everyone's surprise, theistic philosophy was revived.

In 1980 *Time* magazine ran a major story called "Modernizing the case for God." It was about how some of the best and technically most dazzling of contemporary philosophers, people like Alvin Plantinga of Notre Dame University, were doing the unthinkable: defending belief in God. The following sentences from the article are often quoted: "In a quiet revolution in thought and argument that hardly anybody could have foreseen only two decades ago, God is making a comeback. Most intriguingly, this is happening not among theologians or ordinary believers . . . but in the crisp intellectual circles of academic philosophers, where the consensus had long banished the Almighty from fruitful discourse."

Since 1980 that trend or movement has persisted unabated, at least within the domain of analytical philosophy that is given over to the study of things religious, where theistic philosophers are now the largest and most dominant group. Let's call this development "the new theism." (In choosing this label, which, of course, parallels "the new atheism," I am influenced entirely by the recent emergence of both these God-oriented cultural phenomena, not by a negative evaluation of either one.) Working together as they do, theistic philosophers have found their confidence and sense of intellectual security growing. Their books fill the pages devoted to the philosophy of religion in the catalogs of the best university presses, including those of Oxford and Cambridge.

Now, it's not as though the new theism has won a stamp of unalloyed approval from philosophers. Things have changed a bit since the Middle Ages. According to the latest report, 73 percent of philosophers favor atheism. So theists in philosophy as a whole are today a minority group. Most philosophers appear to be of two minds about this group, admiring the technical accomplishment of its best members but regarding the concern for theistic belief with bemusement, seeing it as a sort of foolish obsession supported more by religious observance, in-group loyalty, and a lack of serious exposure to nontheistic ideas (itself fostered by stiflingly one-sided cultural conditions in America, where most new members are generated) than by the true quality of their argumentative case for God. Consequently, the details of that case tend to go unchallenged by them. Indeed, theistic philosophy rarely appears on the radar of most other philosophers today, who are absorbed by their own quite different work, and who generally see a reason to interact with Plantinga and others of his ilk only when—as not infrequently happens—the latter make contributions to ethics, epistemology, or metaphysics that don't require or invite a reference to God. The result is that nontheistic philosophers and theistic philosophers thinking about theism operate in separate worlds, the one group tending to take naturalism for granted and the other recognizing that theism is controversial, but more and more treating it as though it were quite *un*controversial.

Meanwhile—though beginning not in the 1970s or 1980s of the last century but in the first decade of the present one—we've seen a very different "new development" involving discussion of belief in God. This is the new *atheism*, about which I've already had a fair bit to say. Among other reasons for calling this sort of atheism new would be the fact that its advocates, though sharing the naturalism of most philosophers, are, as we've seen, generally moved more by scientific than by philosophical considerations, and, like their leader Dawkins, are often themselves scientists. Concern about the irrationalism of fundamentalist religion and serious irritation over unworthily motivated religious opposition to scientific results, in particular, the theory of evolution, would, as we've seen, have to appear high in the list of factors provoking the rise of the new atheism. Fairly often, being scientists and science-minded people who are vulnerable to an in-group bias of their own, the new atheists display toward philosophy attitudes that are uncomprehending or disparaging.

These tendencies of the new atheists are considerably heightened when it comes to *theistic* philosophers, who are often treated by them as giving aid and sustenance to the enemy, or as belonging to the enemy themselves, and whose detailed arguments tend to be ignored—sometimes after being dismissed as inevitably reflecting bad intellectual motives. And what do theistic philosophers such as Plantinga think of the new atheists? Their attitude resembles the one they would display toward a clever young upstart at the back of a university class who has lots of ideas but lacks the patience to develop them carefully or the humility to recognize their flaws when they are pointed out to him, and so quite avoidably remains at an early stage of development. Indeed, now theistic philosophers in their turn can be found to show an attitude of bemusement, one with trace elements of condescension, which conveys the suggestion that when the required patience and humility have been discovered and sufficiently exercised, there might be something to talk about, but not before.

I'm now going to put on record a few responses to the current state of play involving the new theism. First, its support for belief in God deserves to be seriously and carefully engaged by those many who today are nonbelievers, if only because, like it or not, it represents the furthest and most refined development of one wing of a venerable intellectual tradition stretching back to the Presocratics. Second, a dismissive naturalism is not likely to provide a basis for this. As we've seen, naturalistic philosophers and the new theists tend to pass each other like ships in the night. Third, the arguments against

God of popular atheism (including, in particular, the new atheists) are vulnerable on a number of fronts to refutation by philosophers, whether theist or not, if only because popular atheists have not yet carefully and adequately considered what refutations of their arguments the resources of philosophy might allow. Moreover, as we saw in Chapter 2, a good bit of their work is simply wrongheaded, since grounded in the anti-God idea. Anyone aiming to mount an effective challenge to the new theism needs arguments that will be *hard* for the new theism to refute. Such arguments popular atheism as we see it today seems unable to supply.

To these three points I will now add a fourth, which summarizes what I intend to show in the rest of this chapter. Among the virtues of progressive atheism, an atheism fed by moral progress and defended in the way we've sampled in the last three chapters, is that it could provide the alternative to such weak challengers that the moment demands. As we'll see, because of the nature of the positivity displayed by progressive atheism, some of the dearest emphases of the new theism play right into its hands. In particular, the moral perfection of God is a genuine nonnegotiable for theistic philosophers. Progressive atheism, in short, can provide the basis for the challenge to the new theism that nonbelievers need and should want.

Let me show now how this promise might be fulfilled in relation to what theistic philosophers have recently been emphasizing or assuming.

The "Unsurpassable Greatness" emphasis

There is no doubt that contemporary theistic philosophers owe at least some of their motivation to religious—usually Christian— allegiances, but they also seek to work with integrity as philosophers, often displaying an enviable grasp of philosophy's history. In this they are helped by the fact that, as suggested earlier, there have been Christians in philosophy before the present, indeed *long* before. The first and one of the greatest Christian philosophers was Augustine, whose life straddled the fourth and fifth centuries; and the Middle Ages are chockablock with Christian philosophers.

One of these medieval Christian philosophers, the eleventh-century figure Anselm of Bec (later of Canterbury, because he allowed himself to be talked into becoming archbishop), articulated in a striking way an idea about the nature of any God there may be whose formulation echoes Augustine and also some of the Greeks, a formulation that many theistic philosophers have picked up and are once again running with. In Anselm's own quaint way of putting it, this is—when translated from Latin—the idea that God is that-than-which-a-greater-cannot-be-thought. God, in other words, would have to be unsurpassably great, or the greatest possible being. Philosophers talk about the way of thinking associated with this idea as "perfect being theology."

Using his big idea, Anselm developed what is today called the ontological argument for God's existence. It has seen a lot of new discussion in the last few decades. But many still regard the argument as unsuccessful. Sometimes this is because they disagree with Anselm and modern Anselmians who say that a perfect being, if there were one, would have to exist in all possible worlds. But even those who regard Anselm's argument as unsuccessful can accept Anselm's more fundamental idea, the idea that God would have to be the greatest possible being. They're free to say with David Hume—here recall our discussion in Chapter 3—that it's quite impossible for a concrete thing to inhabit every possible world: a perfect *being* can't be necessary. My point here is that you don't have to go in for everything in perfect being theology, which includes the ontological argument, to accept that God would be a perfect being. That's why so many philosophers, including even atheist philosophers, are able to accept Anselm's basic idea.

And this idea clearly lends itself to progressive atheism. If a God would have to be perfect and the world manifestly is not, or, a bit more subtly, if the world has features incompatible with what a perfect personal being would seek to produce or prevent, then we're off to the races, atheistically speaking. For then precisely through our praise and admiration of the character any God would have we may find reasons to believe that no God exists! Then also we have to give a lot of careful attention to what a perfect personal being would seek to produce or prevent. And so we have to listen up when someone points out that our conception of this is not going to be one and the same, always and forever, but is subject to *evolution*, and that recent and relevant cultural evolutionary developments are pushing the debate decidedly in the direction of atheism.

The first of the points just mentioned most theistic philosophers already appreciate and accept, though while stressing the word "if": *if* the world has features incompatible with what a perfect personal being would seek to produce or prevent, then we're off to the races, atheistically speaking. And, of course, they will argue that in fact the world does not, or does not obviously, have such features. But the second point about moral evolution, central to this book, has been neglected or overlooked by theistic philosophers, as by everybody else. So when it comes to be developed and deployed, as it was in Chapters 4–8, their enthusiasm for Anselm's idea leaves such philosophers without much wiggle room. That second point, as we've seen, can forcefully be used to counter the claim that a perfect personal being could have created our world. And when you add this to the fact that theistic philosophers are forced by their acceptance of Anselm's idea to go along with the first point, you can see that their stance is in danger. Progressive atheists—this is what it comes down to—can claim to turn perfect being theology back on itself.

What we've seen so far, then, is that progressive atheism shows its power to challenge the new theism by *working with its own pro-God emphasis* but coming up with a radically different conclusion. Theistic philosophers are among those especially likely to feel the force of arguments like the ones we developed in previous chapters. (The long-running discussion of the hiddenness problem is testimony to this fact.) Now, having said that, it's also clear that by rejecting the results of moral evolution I have emphasized or their application to God, theists could seek to avoid the atheistic conclusion. But that's very different from *refuting* progressive atheism—showing it to be mistaken. And the cost of backing away from those results is high. You really end up backing into the Middle Ages in a much more conspicuous and disconcerting manner than philosophical theists ever intended when they rediscovered Anselm.

The "Worthiness of Worship" emphasis

Another idea that the new theism has emphasized is the idea that whatever else God may be, God must be worthy of worship, and for most theistic philosophers this means worthy of an unqualified and absolute devotion. Even if Anselm weren't rationally motivating on this subject, their identification with religious communities who, as we saw in Chapter 1, tend to offer God such worship—their attempt to make sense of and to defend the ideas and activities of such religious communities—would make this second idea nonnegotiable for most contemporary theistic philosophers.

Now, there are possible worries about how a person—any person—could be a suitable object of worship, but let's set those aside.

Theistic philosophers have to accept that they can be surmounted. What I want to point out is that with all that we've learned from moral evolution, we'd have to make it a necessary condition of a personal being's worthiness of worship that, in addition to the other personal divine attributes, it possess the dispositions involving relational love, empathy, and nonviolence that are central to the atheistic arguments from hiddenness, horrors, and violence set out in the previous three chapters. (If the possible worries mentioned above became actual it might not be a *sufficient* condition, but all we require is that it be necessary.) A being without these dispositions, or even with contrary dispositions, might force one to bend the knee but it could never elicit adoration. Or, at least, for anyone morally tutored as the human species recently has been this must be the result. But if so, then for a God to be worthy of worship in the relevant sense, God must have attributes that preclude God from existing in the actual world. God is literally *out of this world*, too good for our world. Perhaps in other possible worlds God exists, and we must envy any creaturely denizens of those worlds, but from the actual world a worship-worthy divine being is absent.

Thus, in a second way, we see how precisely in its positive emphasis, the atheism defended in this book can challenge the new theism, showing how an indispensable emphasis of theistic philosophy itself is on its side. Again, theistic philosophers might resist this result by resisting moral evolution, but such an effort would fall short of refutation, at most salvaging the rationality of their own personal believing states. And whether it could even do that much is quite unclear, since we human beings have quietly evolved, morally, in such a way that, when we notice this, we also notice that we have been taking the consequences of moral evolution quite for granted, and have to take responsibility for doing so. It is too late now, for anyone who wants to participate credibly in important mainstream discussions, to disown the assumption that in admirable—let alone worship-worthy—persons we will see empathy, relational love, and nonviolence.

The "Hidden Reasons" emphasis

On record as one of the least helpful things you can say to someone grieving over the tragic loss of a loved one is that we don't know why these things happen, but God must have a reason. Theistic philosophers have recently taken this funeral *faux pas* and turned it into an argument for anyone to consider in a cool hour. This is part of what makes the new theism new. On their view, even if we can't think of a good reason for God to permit events and situations like those enumerated as we developed the hiddenness argument, the argument from horrors, and the argument from violence in the last three chapters—even if, say, moves involving reference to free will or aesthetic value are, as I argued, failures—we have no rational basis to infer that *there is no* good reason. Our grasp of what goods there are, of how they are to be weighed against such things as horrors, and of what logical connections exist between various goods and the worldly phenomena troubling atheists is just too tenuous and limited to make such an inference a safe bet. After all, a God would be omniscient, and we are far from. And even if omnipotent, God can't do logically impossible things, like making 2 + 2 equal 5 or whisking into the world goods that, without horrors, are as impossible as the truth of that equation is. So, for all we know, there are reasons of the required sort. But if God did have a good reason to permit the things that trouble atheists, then God could exist despite them. Therefore, for all we know <u>God *does* exist despite them</u>, which means that any atheistic argument aiming to show otherwise is a failure.

The way of reasoning I've summarized here has won for those theistic philosophers who go in for it—and there are a lot of them—the name *skeptical theists*. Of course, you don't have to be skeptical about everything to accept this reasoning. Nor do you have to be a theist. Theists have been known to point these things out. But most of those who do accept this move are, in fact, theists. And theists will be inclined to use it against atheistic reasoning, including the reasoning we've developed in previous chapters. Does progressive atheism have a good way to challenge it?

At first it might seem that the opposite is true. The emphasis I've placed on human immaturity, which leaves so much room for further evolution and progress, might seem to go rather well with skeptical theism. Our grasp of many things is indeed limited, even if it is improving. But two related and important points should still prevent us from going all the way with skeptical theism, and these can be forcefully developed and pressed by progressive atheists.

First, certain premises of our arguments other than the statement that we can't *think* of good reasons for God to do various things (which I actually haven't used as a premise) logically entail that there *are* no good reasons of the sort for which skeptical theists are holding out hope, and so from some of our results we can infer that skeptical theists must be wrong in these cases. Moreover, these are precisely the claims that have recently been made more obvious by moral progress. Here, to remind you, are the relevant premises from the three arguments (some of them are, in their original settings, first conclusions): if God existed, then there would be no nonresistant nonbelief; a maximally empathetic God who was maximally well acquainted with horrors could not be sufficiently motivated to bring about goods requiring the permission of horrors; and if God existed, then should there be any world at all, it would be some world other than our violent world. Look closely at each of these premises and what you'll see is that if it's true, then there *isn't* a good reason for God to permit the item in question, whether nonresistant nonbelief, horrors, or violence. So here we have one way in which the progressive atheist can turn aside skeptical theism. And because of recent moral evolution, this basis for rejecting skeptical theism has just become a whole lot stronger than it might have seemed to be otherwise, since it is through awareness of this evolution that we have much of our support for those premises. Thus even if before taking account of moral evolution, skeptical theism seemed tempting, it shouldn't do so afterward.

But can we be so sure of ourselves in circumstances of immaturity? Here a second point is important; among other things, it helps to support the first. It is this: immaturity in inquiry makes it sensible for us to focus on things we *can* figure out without residual skepticism even at our early stage of development—and arguably whether there is a divine person is one of them.

Let's develop this idea. The profound term "God" is balanced by the rather accessible term "personal." Yes, the first term has to be seen as always packing a punch. Though the God of Christianity or some other theistic tradition is sometimes spoken of—by believers and by their critics—as if it were a limited being, not much graduated beyond the "old man in the sky" on the ceiling of the Sistine Chapel, it is generally conceived as being quite unlimited and ultimate. But we have to also respect the fact that, sticking with what most theistic thinkers today and certainly the majority of theistic philosophers would say, God is not to be conceived as some vortex of indecipherable profundity but as *personal*—which for them means person-like. Personhood in God is fundamental for traditional theists.

Now, persons we know something about. Sure, the personhood of the theist's God is described with those intimidating "omnis": omnipotence, omniscience, and so on. But omnipotence is power of the sort that persons possess to do things, which God might use to create a universe; and omniscience is knowledge of what's going on, with knowledge too being something all persons can possess, even if it is not knowledge that probes as deeply as God's would do. And, of course, another personal trait God is conceived as possessing—a highly important one because it would determine how God's knowledge and power were used—is moral goodness. We know something about goodness in persons too. So—here's the bottom line—if the idea of God we're concerned with is that of a personal ultimate, then perhaps we have more reason than skeptics think to suppose that our minds are able to get a grip on God. Perhaps there are ideas of transcendent realities too profound for us to get our head around without a lot more intellectual development, but the religious idea at issue here is that of a divine reality who is a *person*, and this seems just the right sort of concept for us to tackle at our present stage of development.

Applying this point, we can observe that each of the atheistic arguments developed in the previous three chapters latches onto personal characteristics, ones with regard to which our understanding has lately been expanded. It would be contrary to the spirit of inquiry not to use what we've been learning and make further progress. Employing that expanded understanding, sensitive to the results of moral evolution, with our focus a modest focus on "subtractions," arguments like those we have developed can yield clear results; and if they do, we should accept these results and seek to build on them, moving further in religious investigation, rather than entertaining the skepticism of skeptical theists.

Here's a way to think about the situation. We know that theists have the courage of their convictions. Philosophical theists are now called upon to have another sort of courage: the courage of their *categories* (or, if you like, the courage of their characterizations). What

I mean is that if you choose the category of a person to use when thinking about the divine, you should live with the results instead of backing off into a skepticism suggesting that you haven't chosen any category at all. Of course, it's entirely possible to say much less about the divine—for example, you might just say that there is some transcendent reality without putting any more into the description than that. But contemporary philosophical theists don't do this. They have proposed a personal divine. They should have the courage of their categories.

Exposing a baseless assumption: The similarity constraint

Perhaps it's appropriate for a form of philosophizing hoping to be true not just to its Christian but to its Greek heritage to have an Achilles's heel. In any case, the new theism apparently has one. Theistic philosophy exposes its vulnerable heel in a baseless assumption that's built into much of the work of its practitioners. Progressive atheism, as we'll see, delivers an arrow to that mark, and its power to challenge theistic philosophy is in yet another way shown when we notice this.

The assumption in question is that God would create a world *might* very similar to ours, right down to the inclusion of physical things and human beings (though not necessarily the human beings who actually exist). Call this the *Similarity Constraint*. What we have here, if less blatant, is not that different from what we were talking about in Chapter 2 when we noted how people may slip creation of the world, the nondivine reality that actually exists, into the definition of "God." Philosophers will speak of God as by definition creator of a universe, meaning a physical universe or multiverse like ours, instead of, correctly, as the creator of any universe there may be. Or they will mistakenly say that God might be expected to be or do such-and-such for *human beings* instead of for such creatures as there may be in any world created by God, whether human or not. All such things signal the influence of the Similarity Constraint.

And how is this assumption woven into the results championed by the new theism? To illustrate, consider skeptical theism once more, in relation to the problem of horrors. Under the influence of the Similarity Constraint people will accept without much reflection that it is, or certainly might be, the case that if there is a God then there exists a world a lot like ours with mountains and trees and human beings and at least some pain and suffering as well. Pain and suffering are easily included because they go rather naturally with physical things and natural laws and human behavior. Of course, if God would produce such a world and permit such evils, then God would have to have good reasons for doing so. And from here theists influenced by the Similarity Constraint may find it's only a short step to the notion that, given the vast differences of power and knowledge between beings like us and a being such as God, if God exists some of God's reasons for evil might be unknown to us or even unknowable—a notion that can be useful when the evils we call horrors become especially troublesome.

I'm not saying that skeptical theism deliberately seeks to bring us to that small step; only that what it does seek to bring us to might be expected to *seem* a small step for someone perhaps unconsciously in the grip of the Similarity Constraint. Indeed, I think the influence of the Similarity Constraint is often not one of which people are fully conscious. How might we have arrived at this point?

In part, I think the answer is to be found in the social contexts of belief and nonbelief. Many of us grow up believing in God, and so we naturally think of God as creating our world. And as suggested in Chapter 2, when atheists come to disbelieve, it is often the God they once thought of in that way (or that they know others think of in that way) to whom their disbelief is directed. Similarly for agnostics who come to be in doubt. Another factor is the very dominance of the new theism in the philosophy of religion today that occasions this chapter. Many contemporary theistic philosophers have always believed in God, and their reflection on the nature of God is therefore quite naturally adapted to the thought that God would create a world like ours. For them, and because of their influence for many others, nothing can be true of God that does not fit with the thought that God would create a physical universe or universes with human beings and many other things like those we experience and see around us.

But I doubt the influence of the first two factors I have mentioned would be so great were it not for a third factor, which is quite simply the *familiarity of the actual*. We can get so used to there being a world of contingent physical things and human beings that the thought of it surreptitiously follows other more explicitly considered ideas into every state we imagine that includes God. Easily we are lulled into thinking of God as the creator of a world like the physical world that science is slowly disclosing to us, instead of more cautiously as the creator of any world there may be.

We need to correct ourselves here, noting that there is nothing in the very nature of God to prevent God from creating a very different world, or perhaps none at all. The idea of God is different in this regard—far more interesting and majestic—than, say, the idea of Santa Claus, which is firmly anchored in the actual, and indeed tied to our planet and its human children. Philosophers should be helping to bring this out. The Similarity Constraint ought to be rejected. It may be difficult to avoid slipping into this assumption. But such an imaginative difficulty is precisely the sort of thing philosophers are committed to overcoming. More to the point, it is an imaginative difficulty that progressive atheism helps us to overcome, by forcing us to think about how different and how much more wonderful would be the behavior of the true God than that of any being who created our world. Even if you don't accept such atheism right off, thinking about it will get you to snap out of the unthinking assumption that God would have to create a world like ours. Liberated from this constraint, people may think of God as having any number of qualities that appear to go with unsurpassable greatness as a person, including ones that would indeed lead to the creation of a very different world, qualities that even theists would have to regard as on the face of it admirable, such as God's finding the permission of horrors or violence entirely out of the question.

Seeing all of this, we'll also see in another way how the new theism is effectively challenged by progressive atheism. After setting aside the Similarity Constraint, we will find many of the arguments of the new theists a lot more controversial than we presently do. Then we will insist, for example, that the skeptical theist and other philosophical theists start a lot further back with the more fundamental and taken-for-granted ideas about a physical world and human beings and evils of some kind, showing that the connections we tend to make between God and the creation or permission of such things are ones atheists or indeed anyone should regard as appropriate. And this it will not be easy to do.

By helping to bring us to this point, and by supporting the other moves we've surveyed in this chapter, progressive atheism can offer a much more pointed and effective challenge to the new theism than other atheisms have it in them to deliver. Other atheistic approaches, including those popular in our culture today, don't have anything like the power of progressive atheism to defend atheistic belief in the face of the best that theistic thought has to offer. They are not able to build on the latter's own emphasis on God as a perfect being or on the worship-worthiness of God. They haven't the way of strengthening atheistic premises that allow for a defeat of skeptical theism. Nor can they diagnose the problem associated with the new theism's Similarity Constraint. Instead of narrowly focusing on the omni-God idea and inviting theists to have the courage of their categories, they make big claims—such as the claim of metaphysical naturalism—that it is much easier for the new theism to hold at bay.

The popularity and influence of the new theism have been growing. It needs to be answered effectively by those who disagree. Any atheist who sees this should want to be a progressive atheist.

10

Atheism's Brave New World

In the novel whose famous title phrase I'm borrowing (Aldous Huxley borrowed it from Shakespeare), the American industrialist Henry Ford and his assembly line have come to represent a societal ideal. Modification and conditioning techniques are utilized to turn out precisely the human products deemed desirable by the World Controllers. Ford himself is treated as a messianic figure, nearly a deity. This is reflected even in ordinary swearing: instead of "My Lord!" people say "My Ford!"

These changes, in Huxley's story, from the time of the historical Ford are brought about through cultural evolution—though it is an example of evolution that most of us would *not* be inclined to view as progressive. (The book is regularly described as "dystopian.") Cultural evolution has changed things a lot in the real world too since 1931, the year Huxley's book was written. And it will likely have changed things a good deal more by the year 2540, in which the book is set. Could progressive atheism contribute to such changes, especially where religion is concerned? Might it evolve further itself, adding to its denial of God curiosity about religious *alternatives* to God and the aim of helping to ensure that future religious changes *do* amount to progress? Might it thus ever more fully grow into its name?

Atheism and progress

I think the answers are all Yes. Let's briefly review the kinds of progress to which that name "progressive atheism" has so far been linked, to provide a context for this new result. There is first of all and most fundamentally moral progress, discussed in Chapters 4 and 5, which makes all the other sorts of progress possible, since on it our approach is based. This is progress that has already occurred. But there is also the progress that might now be made through the use of this approach by atheism: progress for atheism, both within philosophy and without. Such intellectual progress may come from the arguments in Chapters 6–8, and from others in their mold. Moreover there is the more specific sort of progress for atheism that comes from a new ability to handle the new theism both forcefully and effectively. This we discussed in the previous chapter. All these forms of progress for atheism we've understood in part against the background supplied by knowledge of what's lacking in other, presently popular approaches to atheism, whose weaknesses we anatomized in Chapters 2 and 3. Another way of seeing atheism's progress comes from seeing how they *have* been surpassed.

What I'm suggesting as we begin this final chapter is that some additional forms of progress might now be enabled, not so much for atheism as *through* atheism in the wider culture. So far we've been largely concerned with how to get here—with properly identifying the road *to* atheism. But having safely arrived, we may wonder, now what? So there's no omni-God. Where can we go from here? The road from atheism I am recommending will take us into further and deeper religious investigation aimed at informing our future cultural life.

This is, of course, a road from atheism *as reached by our progressive approach*. For anyone still seeking to reach justified atheistic belief from an anti-God or naturalistic perspective, it's likely to appear that the proper follow-up to atheism is putting religion completely out of mind! Atheism's contribution to the wider culture, on these views, is that it leads us *away* from religion and into science. Now, the progressive atheist will certainly support more work in science and the enthusiastic reception of scientific work already done. And as we noticed in Chapter 3, even the development of naturalism as a position in the context of metaphysical discussion (as opposed to its treatment as an assured result) is compatible with progressive atheism. But from atheism reached by a progressive route, more further destinations than these will beckon. Consider again the ethos of progressive atheism, the broader insights about human (im)maturity which it reflects, and the passionate indifference of philosophy by which, above all, it seeks to be motivated. Having absorbed these things, we will find ourselves still interested in nonscientific and non-naturalistic ideas, too—especially those that have not received a full and fair hearing before now. Indeed, the same desire for understanding and impulse to push back our boundaries that led us to atheism will now lead us to explore the contemporary religious landscape much more fully.

It's natural for someone like me who thinks of human inquiry as moving through stages of development to allow broadly historical and cultural factors to influence how *ideas* are treated. I did this in Chapter 1 while getting us ready for our engagement with theism and atheism in this book, and I'm doing it now. The factors that influenced us back in Chapter 1 included the uses to which the omni-God idea has seemed to lend itself in philosophy, its dominant place in God-centered religion, and the ways in which arguments for theism and for atheism have generally been understood in philosophy, all of which has left us with some unfinished business. Much of this book has been devoted to showing how, in our culture as it presently exists, we might finish that business. Progressive atheism, I have argued, helps us reach this result. It would be odd, given everything we've noted about where things stand at our moment in history, and especially given our religious immaturity, for progressive atheism now simply to leave the religious scene. Instead, I suggest, it should be attracted by the *broader* unfinished business of religious investigation.

In the rest of this chapter, I want to provide a kind of map of the zone progressive atheists might undertake to enter and explore on behalf of us all. The map will make little use of familiar categories referring to gods and theisms. Given what we've learned while getting here, it makes sense to seek a way of being oriented in the zone we are now entering that will make new ideas as easy to see as old ones. Since going in will bring challenges, including perhaps a considerable change in its self-image, this is atheism's brave new world.

Vital transmundanity

Arriving at atheism via the progressive route, it may seem that we should immediately launch new investigational expeditions *laterally*—out into other ways of understanding the quite general religious view I called "ultimism" in Chapter 4. We saw there how theism gives ultimism a personal stamp. We also saw how there might be many other ways of providing details for ultimism, including ones yet unnoticed. Maybe we'll be motivated to look for them when we remember our religious immaturity—one feature of which, the cognitive science of religion suggests, may be an evolved bias in favor of agency-oriented and thus personal ideas of the divine.

This would indeed be a good way of promoting the further evolution of progressive atheism I've mentioned. But since the realm of contemporary religious possibilities is a great deal larger than its ultimistic part, I think the first order of business *here* should be getting a good sense of the overall lay of the land. Ultimistic ideas will eventually appear on our map; they occupy a specific, fairly well-defined location. But to begin, we need to take account of even more general notions. And it would be hard to get more general than by considering what some people in the Netherlands known as "ietsers" have recently been talking about.

People who are asked whether they hold conventional religious beliefs will often reply: "No, but there must be *something*." In the Netherlands, this minimalist belief in "something" has been given a name: *ietsisme*—"somethingism." Since 2005 when it was first included in the leading dictionary of the Dutch language, the word has more and more been taken up into other languages, including English, where it appears as "ietsism." And advocates of ietsism are called ietsers.

To make the central idea of "somethingism" a little less vague, it helps to notice that what ietsers have in mind is something *more*. This rather swiftly leads to the question: More than what? Moving cautiously, we might answer "more than the mundane." The mundane in one sense—the sense relevant here—is the ordinary or the everyday, what all of us encounter by doing such things as eating and sleeping and brushing our teeth and going to work. We first approach the religious domain when we think of things that lie beyond—that are more than or other than, even if in various ways entangled with—this familiar realm, common to us all, this realm of the mundane.

But that is still moving very cautiously indeed. Transmundane realities, as we may call them, are found in many and various departments of human life, science and philosophy and art among them. Things can get pretty weird in science and philosophy and art! Think of Duchamp's *Fountain* (an avant-garde work of art consisting largely of a porcelain urinal) or of the Euthyphro dilemma argument in Plato or of Higgs's boson. Not all of us— indeed rather few of us—will get familiar with such things. So they are transmundane. But presumably it would be good to have some way of distinguishing religious realities from just anything in science or philosophy or art.

Perhaps at this point it will occur to us that religious realities are supposed to be able to enrich a whole life—we often speak of "the religious life." They are seen as offering a *way* through life that very importantly adds to its meaning and value. Here the connection between ietsers and those who today see themselves as practicing one or another "spirituality" is illuminating. Note that we needn't be distracted by the misleading designation "spiritual but not religious," which is sensitive only to institutional religiousness. The domain of personal religiousness is broader than that of institutional religiousness. William James, for example, was a deeply religious man—an instance of his own experience was included in his famous book *The Varieties of Religious Experience*—who had little time for organized institutional religion. Indeed, the spread of "spirituality" signals an expansion of the domain of religion in our time.

Now, not just any transmundane reality could be linked to such a spiritual way. That is the thing to notice at this point. Some will be too narrow, too limited in scope, and others too limited in what they can contribute to our lives or too dispensable to function religiously. Think again of Duchamp's *Fountain*. So we are starting to home in on our quarry if we think of transmundane realities that satisfy the extra condition noted here. At least this much we might reasonably expect the ietser who speaks of "something" to go along with: it's something both transmundane and importantly life-enhancing for those who respond appropriately to it. If a label is needed, we might use this one: *vital transmundanity*.

As an account of "religious reality" that will allow us to pin down, definitionally, all religious talk and talk about religion in the history of human culture, what we have here likely won't do: it's still too broad. But as an indication of where we may be going, of the potential flexibility of future thinking about the sort of reality on which a religious life can be focused, I think it deserves our attention. We should be open to it. If different colors indicate, on our map, the different regions of possible religiousness, this could be the base color, present everywhere.

And so in the future it may seem much more natural to regard as a religious reality such things as the most profound type of personal psychic integration or the deepest form of aesthetic insight or the fundamental truth about the nature of reality, whatever it may be (even if it should remain forever mysterious). As you'll probably have noticed, if that's going to be our future, then religiousness will one day be deemed perfectly compatible with naturalistic belief, as, of course, traditional forms of religion, focused on such things as the omni-God idea, clearly are not. Moreover, many different forms of religion may then be compatible with one another, as, again, most traditional forms of religion are not.

Some ideas in this category are more metaphysically ambitious than others. A view known as *emergent theism* suggests that we should think of something like God arising in nature in the future as the eventual result of our universe's growing complexity, much as human and other minds in nature emerged from the physical at some point in the past. If over much time, things in nature became a great deal more interestingly complex, then we might have a reality impressive enough to satisfy various religious purposes without ever leaving the natural realm. And perhaps a form of religiousness in the present is

imaginable that is built on the promotion and/or anticipation of such
future realities.

A very recent idea is still more ambitious, and I'll discuss it at
somewhat greater length just to give a sense of what's possible here.
This view is called *panpsychotheism* (all-minds-are-God-ism).

Proposed by the Purdue philosopher Paul Draper, who agrees
with David Chalmers that we may need "crazy" ideas to solve the
mind-body problem and argues only that we should not rule out
this one, panpsychotheism can with some plausibility be held to do
an impressive number of intellectual jobs, including religious ones,
while staying compatible with naturalism. It even has something like
a God, associated with the notion of a universal consciousness. If
there were such a larger consciousness, which our brains and those
of other creatures and the comparable features of conscious subjects
anywhere in the universe can "use" in something like the way our
 bodies use sunlight, then the problem of how consciousness could
emerge from the material brain goes away. Dualism is also unneeded;
human beings on this view are not a composite of body and soul but
just what the sciences—including the biological sciences—tell us they
are. If, despite being immaterial, this view's "larger consciousness" is
physical by being in space, its existence is compatible with the truth
of naturalism; Draper suggests we think of it as one—but only one—
fundamental feature of nature.

This isn't pantheism. We're not saying that everything is God
but rather that all conscious subjects are part of God—or, more
radically, are identical to God because there is, ultimately, but one
subject of consciousness even if that one subject "demerges" into
multiple agents and persons. It isn't panpsychism either, recently
popularized by the philosopher Galen Strawson, since it doesn't
say that everything is consciousness, down to the tiniest particle in
nature. It isn't panentheism, which regards everything in nature as a

proper part of God and so is not compatible with naturalism. And, of course, it isn't theism, which says that God is distinct from nature and its creator. Not being any of these things, panpsychotheism comes to us without most of their problems. Of course, it has its own problems—but these will be new problems, and they may be interesting and helpful problems, the discussion of which pushes our understanding a bit further. That is something any philosophical atheist should like to see.

To finish the story, let's see how panpsychotheism might also be seen as proposing a *religious* reality fitting our description of the vitally transmundane. Clearly it could promote a profound type of psychic integration! Here, of course, the integration would be *inter*personal, not just personal, and perhaps it would be the more profound and meaningful for that. If the universal mind in this picture is not just the totality of all subjectivity in nature but has its own first-person perspective, then we could even continue to make sense of something like relationship with God. For human beings, there would be the thought that even if we die, the larger reality that contributes the most to who we are—the awareness of which (and of our identification with which) we've been able to heighten through relevant spiritual practice—will continue to exist.

What I've said here is intended only to give a taste of what might be found in the broad domain of ideas concerning vital transmundanity by those who look for it. I'm certainly not saying that any such idea is correct, nor need anyone, like Draper, who develops such an idea say this. Some or all of these ideas might have serious problems. But these are matters for careful investigation, not for hasty prejudicial supposition. By further exploring the possibilities here, anyone might contribute, after atheism, to the fuller, deeper, truth-oriented examination of the religious conceptual domain that we still need.

Triple transcendence

Even if the possibility of naturalistic religion is not set aside as we travel on the other side of atheism, it would be a mistake to suppose that rational religion *must* be naturalistic—that the arc of religiousness, like everything else, with a kind of inevitability bends toward the natural, and that we are the privileged ones who get to see the two touch, to finally make contact. That would assign to naturalism more plausibility than it yet deserves, as we saw in Chapter 3. Instead, we must at this point remind ourselves again of what we saw there about how precisely in relation to religion and so in an area importantly linked to naturalism's claim, human life is implicated in a rather deep form of immaturity-as-shortcoming.

This immaturity has an interesting consequence. What it means is that however implausible existing non-naturalistic religious ideas may be, we need to leave a lot of room on our map for the general religious idea they have sought in varying ways to fill out, which, by entailing that the religious reality transcends nature, entails that naturalism is false. Our immaturity at one and the same time means that, for all we know, naturalism *is* false, and that, for all we know, a far superior filling for the idea of transcendence is waiting for us around some future—perhaps far future—corner.

This idea of transcendence, it should be emphasized, is not *as* general as that of transmundanity. A few colors must now be added. (Of course, the base color remains.) In particular, we need to contemplate a deepening move that turns transmundanity into transcendence, and a sharpening move that articulates the idea's religious content in terms of three forms of transcendence, intertwined.

To get from transmundanity to transcendence, as I am using the terms, we need to think of a reality that would be more than or other than—even if in various ways entangled with—not the mundane realm but the world of nature, as understood by science. Mundane realities are natural but not all natural realities are mundane. As we saw, some are pretty weird. So there can be trans*mundane* realities that are not trans*natural* or (using the more common expression) transcendent. But a transcendent reality by definition in some way surpasses nature. This is why religious ideas that are ideas of a transcendent reality are incompatible with naturalism.

The expression "surpasses nature" could be taken purely in the sense generating the thought that there is more to reality—more facts—if some idea of transcendence is true than otherwise. Something other than nature exists. But what we see in the religious traditions of the world suggests that its existence needs to be related to us in an appropriate way, and this generally includes its being a more fundamental fact about reality than anything in nature. The way the world is—and also the way it is for us—depends in some way on this reality, more so than it depends on any natural fact. For example, there might be a deity who is given power over nature. Plato's demiurge comes to mind. So let's think of the first level of religious transcendence as involving this purely factual quality.

But this is just the first level. To get a clearly religious idea we have to say that a reality of the sort in question would surpass nature in a value-oriented way too. The same intuition that led us to talk of "vitality" in the previous section is at work here. But in this value-oriented side of things we can now distinguish two emphases. First, a transcendent religious reality would be greater in *inherent value* than anything in nature. To do justice to religious emotions we have to say that it would rightly be attractive to us in a way that is captured by speaking of inherent value. Second, and relatedly, it would make available to us and maybe other things in nature as well *a better, deeper, richer life* than is possible given natural means alone. So, here's the notion of a triply transcendent reality in a nutshell: something that <u>transcends nature factually</u>, in inherent value, and in its value for us, for our lives.

Once again we have captured the ietser's idea of "something more," though we have added to what we had before and clarified its content in an appealing way. For it certainly appears that all three forms of transcendence are needed, that the first on its own won't do. If we had only the first, we might not have anything relevant to the provision of meaning and positive value, which we earlier saw religion cannot do without. Even adding the second level of transcendence, though it captures an essential element related to religious attitudes such as awe and worship, seems insufficient since a being that was transcendent factually and in inherent value might <u>still be aloof or out of reach</u>—its value might not be *communicable* to us. Since religion seeks to make divine things accessible, it needs the <u>notion of an accessible</u> divine.

Even if—as the notion of vital transmundanity suggests—religious ideas don't have to be as developed as this idea of triple transcendence, they *may* be. And most important religious ideas of the past *have* been. Consider the idea of gods in ancient Greek religion: they are not in every way constrained by nature's laws and have a lot to do with how things go for humans; they are thought to be in various ways more impressive than things in nature; and you can improve your life in potentially dramatic ways <u>by interacting with them in</u> <u>the right ways.</u> Or, for a radically different example of how one and the same notion can be filled out, take the mysterious Tao of Taoism, which is (metaphorically) Mother of the Ten Thousand Things, wondrous and subtle beyond words, and allows for an analogously wonderful dexterity in the handling of a life in nature for anyone who lives in accordance with the transcendent Tao. Structurally similar descriptions can be given of other religious ideas, including, of course, the idea of one God, whose transcendent power makes possible the creation of heaven and earth and whose transcendent greatness includes a redemptive goodness.

Now, in some of these cases it would be anachronistic to suppose that those who originated the ideas had anything like the concept of triple transcendence themselves; our idea of "nature" had not yet emerged, so there could be no thought of things transcending it. Nonetheless we today can see that what is being thought about *would be* transcendent in the relevant ways if real, and so the language is still appropriate *for us.*

And why should we continue to use it? Why, in particular, should the progressive atheist feel any need to investigate such possibilities further? Again, the answer begs to be given in terms of our immaturity. There are ideas of triple transcendence that have received scant attention before now, including ideas of a personal deity with something other than "omni" characteristics. The process ideas mentioned in Chapter 1 and various associated or similar views, such as panentheism, which has it that the world is in God, are among them.

The Australian philosopher Peter Forrest, explicitly aiming to provide an alternative to theism as we've generally known it, has recently put forward an inventive variation on such themes. He calls it *developmental theism.* His work shows how, without going in for the idea that processes are metaphysically fundamental, one can still explore the idea of a godlike being who changes and grows over time—in Forrest's proposal, from a calculating utility-maximizer to unbounded love. A God of this sort, even if it starts out with no more than the first sort of transcendence, might *become* triply transcendent. One of Forrest's intriguing ideas is that, not being furnished with omni-attributes, such a being might, even after it's religiously well-developed, have to work within the constraints set by its *earlier* decisions. This provides a way of understanding how our world could be less than

Woody Allan's
Underachiever

perfectly conducive to human well-being even if its creator is *now* as loving as one might want. Forrest's God represents one way of arriving at a notion like that advanced already in the nineteenth century by John Stuart Mill, which he suggested we might reasonably hope is true—the idea of a less than infinite supreme being who struggles with us for a future state much more friendly to humanity and other creatures than many past states of the world have been. The difference in Forrest's idea is that those past states include the deity's own!

Such ideas as these or new ideas along this front including ideas less tied to the notion of a personal reality than Mill's and Forrest's still are—perhaps ones taking their inspiration from non-Western creations such as Taoism—may beckon to philosophers as the idea of an omni-God recedes. Further investigations of progressive atheism should have room for them.

It's interesting to contemplate how the various existing religious ideas of transcendence, even if all mistaken (and, of course, more investigation would be needed to establish that), might be mistaken not in postulating a triply transcendent reality but rather in the *details* they add to flesh that idea out. Perhaps progressive atheism can discover other details. If so, we would do well to determine whether they must meet the same fate. And, in any case, the idea of triple transcendence alone deserves more scrutiny, for example, in relation to the concept of a religious life. In view of the repeated "t" and with a wink in the direction of theism, we might call the bare claim that there is a triply transcendent reality of some kind *t-ism*. Might t-ism on its own, without any filling at all, provide a basis for religious living? Could this be an appropriate way for humans to live religiously at an early and immature stage of religious development? Would any suggestion that we *ought* to retreat from transcendence to something like transmundanity reflect, again, an inadequate sense of our religious immaturity and naturalism's vulnerability?

Triple ultimacy

With these questions and possibilities still buzzing in our ears, let's now add one more location—one more religious region—to our map. Again some extra color will be needed. In particular, we need to take account of the fact that we're moving from the notion of transcendence to that of *ultimacy*. Religious ultimacy includes transcendence, just as transcendence includes transmundanity, but it *adds* something— something found in many existing religious ideas and perhaps also in many ideas with which our species has not yet become acquainted.

What it adds is depth. If a transcendent reality is deeper, more fundamental, than nature, an ultimate reality may be deeper still and indeed must be the deepest possible. It is as deep as you can go. And triple ultimacy is unsurpassable depth in all three of the categories we distinguished when talking about triple transcendence: to be triply ultimate something has to be ultimate factually, and in inherent value, and in its value for us—for our lives. In other words, its existence is the deepest, most fundamental reality, it is possessed of the deepest possible inherent value, and at the same time it is the source of our deepest good. We saw in the previous section why all three categories are religiously significant. The only difference when speaking of ultimacy is that all the limits are taken away.

Here we have in a way come full circle, since, as noted a couple of sections ago and in Chapter 4, among the existing religious ideas that are triply ultimistic is the idea that most of this book has been about: the omni-God idea of theism. If there is such a God, its existence is not just a transcendent fact but the ultimate fact. The omni-God is also—precisely by virtue of those omnis—regarded as unsurpassably great. And it's hard to imagine a deeper good for ourselves than being loved by a God so great who is our creator, especially if we have been created *for* such love. An atheist, of course, holds that no such God exists—that personal ultimism is false. What the progressive atheist is now called to notice and take seriously, however, is that other ways in which triple ultimacy might be said to be realized are waiting to be explored. Perhaps one of them is true even if theism is false.

Here's a mistake to watch out for at this point. It would be easy to suppose that if *personal* ultimism is false, then the progressive atheist, insofar as she is continuing to explore ultimistic regions of religiousness, will have to concern herself with *im*personal versions or elaborations of ultimism. But this doesn't follow. We called theism by that name, "personal ultimism," because everything in the elaboration is constrained by—kept within—the category of the personal. Everything. God *is* a person or something like a person; all God's attributes, accordingly, are personal ones. So not just impersonal versions of ultimism *but also any elaboration that doesn't make the personal that fundamental* will count as an alternative to personal ultimism. "Nonpersonal" is the adjective we need, not "impersonal."

Consider, for example, an idea suggested by the seventeenth-century Dutch philosopher Baruch Spinoza. Spinoza was kicked out of the Jewish religious community in which he grew up for espousing what seemed to its other members like serious heresy. For one thing, Spinoza seemed to deny any real distinction between God and the world or what he called Nature. He's regularly cited as a pantheist for this reason. And Western religious traditions such as Judaism have not always taken kindly to pantheism. But Spinoza's God/Nature is apparently not the nature of the naturalist. It is "a being absolutely infinite, i.e., a substance consisting of an infinity of attributes, of which each one expresses an eternal and infinite essence." And the physical, which for the naturalist is enough to comprehend reality, represents for Spinoza just one out of *an infinite number* of divine "modes" or ways of being. Even if you added the mental or mind, thinking of this as distinct from the physical (and thus also comprehending the realm of the personal, on any conception of it), you'd still only have *two* out of Spinoza's infinite number of divine modes. Talk about a limitless idea!

So here—or at least suggested here—is a view that includes personal attributes *within* a vastly larger reality. The personal, which the theist takes to be ultimate on its own, a Spinozist might view as occupying a position something like the single numeral "3" in a page of Einstein's equations. But it is included. The view is nonpersonal, not impersonal.

Moreover, here we have an idea that provides a way of thinking about triple ultimacy. An eternal and infinite and infinitely rich reality might be said to satisfy all three conditions: nothing could be more fundamental than the fact of its existence, nothing more inherently valuable than what it encompasses, and, in part for these reasons, nothing could be better for us than ordering our life in a way that lines up with these facts.

What this might mean in practice and in detail would depend on the details that are added to the view. Spinoza himself was a determinist, so he recommended knowing and accepting our place in Nature, using our knowledge to still the unruly passions, and cultivating an intellectual love of God that, so he thought, brings both serenity and—with every improvement in the quality of our ideas—a fuller participation in God's attribute of thought, where something of us accordingly remains when we die. But by experimenting with other details we would no doubt generate different prescriptions, different understandings of how one might turn a kind of pantheism into an ultimistic way.

What I've said here is once again intended only to give a taste of what progressive investigators may find in the broad religious terrain—this time in its ultimistic regions. But why travel to these peaks at all? The Western preoccupation with an omni-God idea explains why we have had the unfinished business that atheistic arguments seek to finish. And the omni-God idea is ultimistic. But having left that idea behind, and now having seen how the religious domain includes so much more, including triple transcendence (which doesn't have to be ultimistic, and even vital transmundanity, which can manage without transcendence) why would anyone choose to linger in this other area, where the air is thin and the climb steep?

Well, why have humans ever been drawn to peaks and ambitious, dangerous climbing? I suspect one good reason would come just from answering that question. Humans have often shown a kind of yearning for the infinite, in religion at least as much as anywhere else. Ultimistic views propose to satisfy that yearning. And we might propose to investigate them to see how far we can go in this climb. It would certainly be important if some other form of ultimism did better than personal ultimism could do. And, given our religious immaturity, we have to take seriously the idea that much more is possible, in the pursuit of fact and value blended and infinitized, than might at first appear to be. So what *if* the naturalists are wrong and in place of nature we have Nature to contend with?

Various ways of configuring ultimism we should, of course, expect there to be, and new ones may emerge as our species develops further. But much as in the case of what I called t-ism, even if none proved adequate, the general view of ultimism itself, the simple view focused on triple ultimacy alone, might remain, significantly uneliminated, in an age when we are struggling to overcome religious immaturity. Even if a specific elaboration of ultimism such as the theism discussed in this book is provably false, about ultimism itself we may be able to justify no more nor less than doubt. And as a number of philosophers have recently been arguing, some religious attitudes—including even a kind of religious faith—can be combined with doubt. Thus ultimism alone might provide guidance for future religious lives, even if we think no human view yet developed, and perhaps no human view ever developed, can fill it out adequately. The rational propriety of such religious lives would be quite compatible with the truth of atheism.

Now, progressive atheism may well eventually take human beings elsewhere, even into a confirmed naturalism. But it behooves us at this point to notice how, before a proper, thorough investigation of the vast domain of religion we've been mapping has *actually been undertaken*, the possibility of even unusual and unexpected religious results must remain wide open.

A positive vision

Ludwig Wittgenstein, whom we first encountered in Chapter 1, said, as I mentioned there, that we should always be willing to see our problems as though for the first time. Here's another thought he jotted into his notebook: "In philosophy the winner of the race is the one who can run most slowly. Or: the one who gets there last." Both thoughts should resonate with us as we finish this book.

Seeing atheism as though for the first time, we may see a negative result on the omni-God idea as only the first step in a long journey. Our culture's unfinished business, where religion is concerned, still stretches out before us like a vast unexplored country. A new world. Only the immature tendencies of human beings both inside and outside religion have obscured it from us. Mobilizing the attitudes of philosophy, including its passionate indifference, we won't yield to the temptation to write off religious ideas with a denigrating comment or two about human religion as we've known it so far, or swiftly dismiss all such ideas in the name of naturalism. Atheism, we'll say, for all we know may come at the *beginning* of religion rather than the end.

But if we should go slow, why close off even the possibility of a personal omni-God? Why atheism at all, which clearly is negative—even if nonevaluatively—about the prospect of God's existence, rather than agnosticism, which isn't?

There is indeed a negative quality here, and it could even graduate to the status of an evaluative negativity if—as I think it should—it leads us to evaluate negatively the value of further investigation into the existence of the omni-God. How can this be defended? *By exposing the larger positive cultural result which this negativity allows.* Denial of the existence of God, as understood in this book, may, in any case, seem unavoidable for anyone who takes the measure of arguments like those we've discussed, but he will not be afraid to advance the cause of such a denial in the public forum if he notices that by so doing he is making room for other understandings of the world to receive the investigation that is their due. So the negativity appears in the context of positivity. These additional understandings, of course, include naturalism but, as we've seen in this chapter, they also include many actual and possible understandings of a religious reality other than the exclusively personalist ones that have dominated human religion to this point. Who knows how much more there will be to see and know when the idea of God has been set aside?

When thinking about whether the denial of God's existence, rather than a suspense of judgment about the matter, can at our stage of development be justified, we are thinking of how properly to strike a balance—a balance between the demands of openness to new and surprising results and the need to get results! Here we see that it is precisely by accepting as a result of inquiry that there is no personal omni-God that progressive atheism is able to be progressive in the sense of moving us on to other regions of possibility. Especially given what we saw in the last chapter about the importance of having the courage of our categories, I think such an attitude gets the balance right.

Who knows how much more there is to see and know? That, at bottom, is what drives a progressive atheism that fully embodies the approach set out in this book, now including the previous sections of this chapter. What we have here is, in the end, a positive vision of how much remains for us to explore and how much deeper we need to go. Though intellectually oriented, a more thoroughgoing honesty and, yes, bravery will be required to live out this vision. More intertwined intellectual and moral growing will be demanded of us all.

Imagine a day when such larger ambitions, and not just atheism's denial of theism, come to mind for people when the word "atheism" is spoken. Atheism will then quite naturally be paired with high moral expectations. It will be seen as interested in probing every evolutionary frontier. Then we'll trust atheism to be as hard on itself as it is on other orientations—to look only for the truth, whatever that may be, without insisting that the truth should speak with this or that particular inflection. We'll think of atheism as willing to conclude that *all* religious ideas, like the idea of the personal omni-God, end up going nowhere, but as being ready also for insights showing there to be a kind of religious truth that wonderfully smashes everyone's preconceptions. In all its doings, atheism will be pushing us forward, always restlessly forward, toward what is higher, truer, purer, and more worthy of human contemplation.

We're not there yet. But the growing continues.

Notes

Preface

p. viii: That's because I've defended. My earlier arguments for atheism appear in various places. One is *The Wisdom to Doubt*, part III.

p. viii: This is the larger part of what I've done. See, in particular, my trilogy from Cornell, which includes *The Wisdom to Doubt*, already mentioned, but also *Prolegomena to a Philosophy of Religion* (2005) and *The Will to Imagine: A Justification of Skeptical Religion* (2009).

p. viii: I had appealed to *divine* empathy. The reasoning mentioned here appears in *The Wisdom to Doubt: A Justification of Religious Skepticism* (Ithaca, NY: Cornell University Press, 2007), Chapter 11.

p. ix: The hiddenness argument for atheism I had developed. This argument first appeared in *Divine Hiddenness and Human Reason* (Ithaca, NY: Cornell University Press, 1993). It was updated for a general audience in *The Hiddenness Argument: Philosophy's New Challenge to Belief in God* (Oxford: Oxford University Press, 2015).

Chapter 1

p. 1: Born into one of the wealthiest families of Europe. My information on Wittgenstein's life comes largely from the excellent biography by Ray Monk, *Ludwig Wittgenstein: The Duty of Genius* (New York: Penguin, 1990).

p. 2: As the nineteenth-century British philosopher and social reformer John Stuart Mill wrote. This famous line of Mill's appears in *Utilitarianism*. See *The Collected Works of John Stuart Mill*, John M. Robson, gen. ed. (Toronto: University of Toronto Press, 1963–91), vol. X, p. 212.

p. 3: Certainly many books have been written about Wittgenstein's reasoning. See, for example, Saul A. Kripke, *Wittgenstein on Rules and Private Language*, rev. ed. (Cambridge, MA: Harvard University Press, 1984) and Colin McGinn, *Wittgenstein on Meaning* (London: Blackwell, 1984).

p. 6: At least since Charles Darwin's friend Thomas Huxley came up with the term. Huxley's claim about his invention appears in Leonard Huxley, ed. *The Life and Letters of Thomas Henry Huxley*, vol. I (London: Macmillan, 1900), pp. 319–20.

p. 10: Deeply influenced by the thinking of the British philosopher Alfred North Whitehead. Whitehead's great work is *Process and Reality*. See the corrected edition, edited by David Ray Griffin and Donald W. Sherburne (New York: The Free Press, 1978).

p. 11: Process theists emphasize their altered and attenuated understanding of God's *power*. See, for example, David Ray Griffin, *God, Power, and Evil: A Process Theodicy* (London: Westminster John Knox Press, 2004).

Chapter 2

p. 23: Something said by the well-known philosopher Thomas Nagel. For these comments of Nagel, see his book *The Last Word* (New York: Oxford University Press), pp. 130–31.

p. 26: He famously describes the God of the first 70 percent of the Bible. See Richard Dawkins, *The God Delusion* (Boston, MA: Houghton Mifflin Harcourt, 2006), p. 51.

p. 29: An example is found in the writing of Richard Carrier. Carrier's thoughts may be found here: https://www.richardcarrier.info/archives/11007.

p. 31: They're in the position of John Stuart Mill. Mill's statement about never having had religious belief appears in his *Autobiography*. See *The Collected Works of John Stuart Mill*, John M. Robson, gen. ed. (Toronto: University of Toronto Press, 1963–91), vol. I, p. 45.

Chapter 3

p. 38: As the philosopher Colin McGinn suggests. *Problems in Philosophy: The Limits of Inquiry* (Oxford: Blackwell, 1993), p. 14.

p. 39: **But as the philosopher David Hume pointed out**. For the Humean
points raised in this paragraph, see Part IX of his *Dialogues Concerning
Natural Religion*, Richard H. Popkin, ed. (Indianapolis, IN: Hackett, 1998).

p. 48: **In one such experiment**. See Daniel Kahneman, *Thinking: Fast and Slow*
(New York: Penguin, 2011), pp. 125–26.

p. 48: **The reviewer of a Kahneman essay collection in 1984 was able to point
out**. J. Scott Armstrong, "Review of Daniel Kahneman, Paul Slovic, and
Amos Tversky (eds.), *Judgment Under Uncertainty: Heuristics and Biases*,"
Journal of Forecasting 3 (1984), 235–39.

p. 48: **Ideology and prejudice are sometimes causally linked to cognitive
biases**. See, for example, John T. Jost, Sally Blount, Jeffrey Pfeffer, and
György Hunyady, "Fair Market Ideology: Its Cognitive-Motivational
Underpinnings," in Barry M. Staw and Roderick M. Kramer, eds., *Research
in Organizational Behavior: An Annual Series of Analytical Essays and
Critical Reviews*, vol. 25 (Greenwich, CT: JAI Press, 2003), pp. 53–91 and
Sarah-Jane Leslie, "The Original Sin of Cognition: Fear, Prejudice, and
Generalization," *The Journal of Philosophy* 114 (2017), 393–421.

p. 49: **Robert M. Sapolsky makes a point**. See Robert M. Sapolsky, *Behave: The
Biology of Humans at Our Best and Worst* (New York: Penguin, 2017), p. 605.

p. 56: **As Bertrand Russell once said**. For the famous quip, see Bertrand
Russell, *Introduction to Mathematical Philosophy* (London: Routledge, 1919),
p. 71.

Chapter 4

p. 62: **The philosopher Philip Kitcher goes quite a bit further back**. The
Kitcher examples are taken from his book *The Ethical Project* (Cambridge,
MA: Harvard University Press, 2011), pp. 140–65. Kitcher's reference to the
"withering of vice" appears on p. 162.

p. 64: **All the reductions in violence to be associated with a host of recent
"Rights Revolutions" focused on "civil rights . . . "** Steven Pinker, *The
Better Angels of Our Nature: Why Violence Has Declined* (New York: Viking),
p. 380.

p. 65: **The slow roasting of wailing cats was considered good clean fun**.
Pinker, *Better Angels*, p. 145.

p. 66: **Contemporary work on the subject.** See Tim Lewens, *Cultural Evolution* (Oxford: Oxford University Press, 2015) and also Peter Richerson and Robert Boyd, *Not by Genes Alone: How Culture Transformed Human Evolution* (Chicago, IL: University of Chicago Press, 2005).

p. 71: **Pinker suggests that the issue we've raised is a kind of pseudo-issue.** See Steven Pinker, *Enlightenment Now: The Case for Reason, Science, Humanism, and Progress* (New York: Viking, 2018), pp. 51–52.

p. 75: **A white cross still hangs on the dirty back wall.** I read the story of Ireland's infamous Magdalene laundries here: https://www.nytimes.com/2018/06/06/world/europe/magdalene-laundry-reunion-ireland.html.

Chapter 5

p. 93: **When two self-declared atheists . . . stopped by for lunch and a chat in his study.** One of them, Aveling, wrote up an account of the event later that year in *The Religious Views of Charles Darwin* (London: Freethought Publishing Company, 1883).

p. 93: **Darwin claimed his friend Huxley's newly minted label "agnostic" for himself.** See Janet Browne, *Charles Darwin: The Power of Place* (Princeton, NJ: Princeton University Press, 2002), p. 391.

p. 94: **One of his final acts.** The Darwin beetle story is told by David Quammen, *The Reluctant Mr. Darwin* (New York: W. W. Norton, 2006), pp. 252–53.

Chapter 6

p. 102: **The following principle is applicable here.** I first articulated this principle in *The Hiddenness Argument*, pp. 44–45. This is the book to choose if you're looking for a fuller discussion of the hiddenness argument aimed at a general audience.

Chapter 7

p. 109: **The theologian Hans Küng has called it the "rock of atheism."** See Hans Küng, *On Being a Christian*, Edward Quinn, trans. (Garden City, NY: Doubleday, 1976), p. 432.

p. 110: Alvin Plantinga relating the true story of a man who accidentally crushes his own small child. See Plantinga's "Self-Profile," in Peter van Inwagen and James E. Tomberlin, eds., *Alvin Plantinga* (Dordrecht: Reidel, 1985), p. 34.

p. 110: Marilyn McCord Adams describes. Adams's example of horrendous suffering and her definition of the concept appear in her book *Horrendous Evils and the Goodness of God* (Ithaca, NY: Cornell University Press, 1999), p. 26.

p. 111: Pinker interestingly suggests that one of them was a sharp increase in novel reading. See *Better Angels*, pp. 174–75.

p. 112: We have to attribute to God the capacity for such awareness. I argued that our concept of omniscience needs to be expanded in this way in Chapter 11 of *The Wisdom to Doubt*, where an earlier version of this chapter's atheistic argument also appeared. Linda Zagzebski independently made much the same point about God's awareness in "Omnisubjectivity," in Jon Kvanvig, ed., *Oxford Studies in Philosophy of Religion*, vol. 1. (Oxford: Oxford University Press, 2008).

Chapter 8

pp. 130–131: What John Hick, borrowing from John Donne, has called "soul-making." Hick develops this idea in many places. A concise and relatively recent presentation is in his book *An Interpretation of Religion* (London: Macmillan, 1989), chapter 7.

p. 131: As Richard Swinburne has suggested. See his *The Existence of God*, 2nd ed. (Oxford: Clarendon Press, 2004), Chapters 10 and 11.

p. 133: An aesthetic reason. I am indebted to Paul Draper for getting me to take this kind of reason more seriously. He discusses some related issues in "What If God Makes Hard Choices?" *Oxford Studies in Philosophy of Religion*, vol. 9 (Oxford: Oxford University Press, 2018).

Chapter 9

p. 138: Since 1980 that trend or movement has persisted unabated. And the result is that the Society of Christian Philosophers now has well over a thousand members, making it one of the largest philosophical societies in the United States. This has been reported for some time now, most recently (as far as I can tell) in Mark A. Tietjen, *Kierkegaard: A Christian Missionary to Christians* (Downers Grove, IL: InterVarsity Press, 2016), p. 34.

pp. 138–139: According to the latest report, 73 percent of philosophers favor atheism. See David Bourget and David J. Chalmers, "What Do Philosophers Believe?" *Philosophical Studies* 170 (2014), 476.

Chapter 10

p. 159: In the Netherlands, this minimalist belief in "something" has been given a name: *ietsisme* – "somethingism." As far as I can tell, no substantial discussion has yet appeared in print, but here is some relevant internet discussion: https://www.kuleuven.be/thomas/page/ietsisme/.

p. 161: A view known as *emergent theism*. See Samuel Alexander, *Space, Time, and Deity* (London: Macmillan, 1920) and Anthony Freeman, "God as an Emergent Property," *Journal of Consciousness Studies* 8 (2001), 147–59.

p. 162: Proposed by the Purdue philosopher Paul Draper. See his "Panpsychotheism," in *Current Controversies in Philosophy of Religion* (New York: Routledge, 2019).

p. 162: Recently popularized by the philosopher Galen Strawson. See, for example: https://www.nybooks.com/daily/2018/03/13/the-consciousness-deniers/.

p. 167: Peter Forrest, explicitly aiming to provide an alternative to theism. See his *Developmental Theism: From Pure Will to Unbounded Love* (Oxford: Clarendon Press, 2007).

p. 168: A notion like that advanced already in the nineteenth century by John Stuart Mill. See the second and third of his *Three Essays on Religion*, 4th ed. (London: Longmans, Green, Reader, and Dyer, 1875).

p. 170: "A being absolutely infinite, i.e., a substance consisting of an infinity of attributes, of which each one expresses an eternal and infinite essence." Spinoza, *The Ethics*, Part 1, definition 6.

p. 173: "In philosophy the winner of the race is the one who can run most slowly. Or: the one who gets there last." Ludwig Wittgenstein, *Culture and Value*, Peter Winch trans. (Chicago, IL: University of Chicago Press, 180), 34c.

Glossary

atheism The view that God does not exist

biological evolution The processes of change in nature associated with Charles Darwin and his idea of natural selection

cultural evolution The processes of change in human culture guided in part by human effort and not necessarily involving natural selection or any analogous mechanism

evil Anything bad, whether intentionally caused or not, especially including pain and suffering

God A personal divine being who is all-powerful (or omnipotent), all-knowing (or omniscient), and the morally perfect creator of any universe there may be; also referred to as the omni-God

horrors The worst instances of suffering, which give to those who experience or perpetrate them a reason to think their life not worth living

ietsism The view, popular in the Netherlands and increasingly elsewhere, that even if the formulations of traditional religion fail to capture its nature, there is "something more"

immaturity-as-potential The state of being in some respect undeveloped but liable to reach a developed condition in the future; seen not just in people but in many things that can change over time

immaturity-as-shortcoming The state of being in some respect undeveloped because of behavior in the past that has prevented development or delayed it

metaphysical naturalism The view that nature, explored by science, is the only reality

moral evolution The aspect of cultural evolution involving changes in our conception of what it takes to be a "really good person"

necessary being A being that exists in just any possible state of affairs, and so cannot *not* exist

nonresistant nonbelief An absence of belief in God that is not caused by resistance of God on the part of the nonbeliever

omnibenevolence The attribute of God, associated with God's moral perfection, that consists in having the greatest possible concern for the good of others

omni-God God as understood by reference to such omni-attributes as omnipotence, omniscience, and omnibenevolence

perfect being theology The field of inquiry, part of contemporary philosophy of religion, that involves an attempt to solve problems about the nature and existence of God by applying Anselm's idea that God is a perfect being: that-than-which-a-greater-cannot-be-thought

Philosopher's God God as commonly understood in philosophy; the omni-God

Presocratics The first philosophers in the West, who lived and worked in ancient Greece over (roughly) the 200-year period prior to the rise of Socrates (whose own dates are 470–399 BCE)

Similarity Constraint The assumption, commonly found in contemporary philosophy of religion, that any world God might create would be similar to our world, right down to its physical nature and the presence in it of human beings

skeptical theism The view, popular in contemporary philosophy of religion, that we cannot rule out but should rather be in doubt about whether there are good states of affairs, unknown to us, that justify God in permitting horrors or remaining hidden from us

theism The view that God exists

transcendent The state of being in some way more than or other than the world of nature studied by science

transmundane The state of being in some way more than or other than the ordinary or the everyday or the mundane dimension of life, which all of us encounter by doing such things as eating and sleeping and brushing our teeth and going to work

ultimate The deepest or greatest possible in some respect—as, for example, in an explanation of the nature of reality or in value

ultimism The view that there is a transcendent reality ultimate in three ways: in reality, in inherent value, and in its potential contribution to our good and that of the world. (As the corresponding terms are defined here, ultimism and atheism are compatible.)

violence An activity or event involving the application of harsh and rude force to a sensitive being, rather than gentleness and respect; conceptually distinct from suffering

Acknowledgments

I am most grateful to the authors of several anonymous reports on my manuscript solicited by Bloomsbury for comments that helped to shape the final version of the book, and to my editor at the Press, Colleen Coalter, for exceptionally friendly and insightful guidance at various stages along the way. I also want to thank Paul Draper, whose extensive comments on a draft of the book illuminated many issues and helped me to see where more work was needed. My wife and best friend, Regina Coupar, has, as ever, been a most valuable critic, patiently listening to my words and incisively commenting on how they might more effectively be bent to my purposes. This book is dedicated to her with the deepest gratitude and affection.

Index

Adams, Marilyn McCord   110
Advaita Vedanta   54
aesthetic value   133–5
agnosticism, defined   6–7
Anaxagoras   19, 36, 61, 137
Anselm   142–4
arguments, defined   3
Aristotle   17
Armstrong, Karen   85–6
atheism, defined   5
Atomism   18–19, 36, 52–3
Augustine   142
Aveling, Edward B.   93

belief, nature of   104
biological evolution   xi, 54,
      59–61, 67, 78, 89, 106, 126,
      127. *See also* Darwin, Charles
Boyd, Robert   66
Büchner, Ludwig   93
Buddha   35

Carrier, Richard   29
Chalmers, David   162
cognitive biases   47–8
cognitive science of
      religion   37, 158
consciousness, problem
      of   38–9, 50

cultural evolution   x, 61, 67, 71,
      98, 107, 133, 136, 143, 155,
      173–4
   distinguished from cultural
      progress   66

Darwin, Charles   6, 57, 59, 89, 92–5,
      97–8, 133
Dawkins, Richard   26, 139
Dennett, Daniel   2
developmental theism   167–8
Donne, John   131
Draper, Paul   162–3
Duchamp's *Fountain*   160

Einstein, Albert   171
emergent theism   161
empathy   viii, 64, 65, 66, 69, 87,
      110–17, 146
evil, problem of   ix, 29, 109–21,
      151

Ford, Henry   155
Forrest, Peter   167–8
free will   128–33

Gandhi, Mahatma   65, 87,
      115, 123
God, defined   4

Hick, John   130–1
hiddenness argument   ix, xi, 13,
      97–108
Hitler, Adolph   22
horrors, defined   109–10
Hume, David   39, 142
Huxley, Aldous   155
Huxley, Thomas   6, 93

ietsism   159–60, 166

James, William   160
Jesus of Nazareth   44, 65, 90

Kahneman, Daniel   48
Kant, Immanuel   68
King, Jr., Martin Luther   65,
      87, 123
Kitcher, Philip   62–3, 120
Küng, Hans   109

Lewens, Tim   66, 67
Lincoln, Abraham   65, 87
love, nature of   97–8

McGinn, Colin   38–9
Magdalene laundries   75–6
masculine prejudice   ix, 47, 50, 64,
      87, 90, 98–9
maturity/immaturity of
      inquiry   43–56, 72–5,
      147–50, 157, 158, 164, 172
Mennonites   123–4, 127
Mill, John Stuart   2, 12, 31, 168
moral evolution, defined   x
moral progress   x, 62–76, 78, 86–8,
      93, 116, 125, 135, 156
   defined   71
moral theories   68–70
Mother Teresa   115

Nagel, Thomas   23–5, 26, 27
naturalism   20–3, 33, 35–57, 139,
      140, 154, 157, 162, 163, 164–5,
      173, 174
   distinguished from
      atheism   35
new atheism   12, 25–6, 32,
      139–40. *See also* popular
      atheism
new theism   137–54, 156
Nightingale, Florence   65, 87, 91

Orwell, George   126

panentheism   162–3
panpsychism   162
panpsychotheism   162–3
pantheism   162, 170–1
Paul, the apostle   77–8
perfect being theology   142–4
philosophy, nature of   2–4
Pinker, Steven   viii, 64–5, 71, 73,
      111
Plantinga, Alvin   110, 138,
      139, 140
Plato   17, 61, 165
popular atheism   ix, 78, 141,
      153–4, 156. *See also* new
      atheism
Presocratics   17–19, 61
process philosophy   10–11, 167
progressive atheism, defined   xi–xii,
      156

religious evolution   85–92
religious experience   9, 40, 52,
      101–2
Richerson, Peter   66
Roosevelt, Eleanor   65–6, 87, 91
Russell, Bertrand   56

Sapolsky, Robert M.   49
science   3, 12, 15, 17, 20, 26, 37–8,
    40, 41, 45, 49, 50, 53, 55–6,
    67, 68, 73, 129, 130, 139–40,
    157. *See also* biological
    evolution
  timescales of   38, 41–2,
    43–5
sexism. *See* masculine prejudice
Shakespeare   155
similarity constraint   150–4
skeptical theism   146–50
Socrates   2, 12, 17, 61
Spinoza, Baruch   170–1
spirituality   160
Swinburne, Richard   131

Tao   166
theism, defined   5

transcendence, defined   164–5
  triple, defined   165–6
transmundane, defined   159
Tversky, Amos   48

ultimacy   4, 8–9, 26, 79–81, 169–72
ultimism   80, 158, 170, 172

violence   64–5, 73, 74, 87, 123–36
  distinguished from pain and
    suffering   124–5

Waismann, Friedrich   2
Whitehead, Alfred North   10
Wiesel, Elie   65–6, 87, 116
Wittgenstein, Ludwig   1–2, 3, 12,
    15, 173
women   47, 63, 64, 70, 75, 87
worship   8, 11, 144–6